STORYBOOK
Connections
Fairy Tale Activities from A to Z

I'm late!

sin

by Mary Bannister
illustrated by Philip Chalk

Publisher: Roberta Suid
Design: Jeffrey Goldman
Copy Editor: Carol Whiteley
Production & Typesetting: Santa Monica Press

Other books in this series: *Alphabet Connections* (MM 1969)
and *Preschool Connections* (MM 1993).

For a complete catalog, please write to the address below:
P.O. Box 1680, Palo Alto, California 94302

Monday Morning is a registered trademark of
Monday Morning Books, Inc.

ISBN
1-878279-78-5

Printed in the United States of America

987654321

CONTENTS

Introduction   4

How to Use This Book   5

A: Alice's Adventures in Wonderland   7

B: Beauty and the Beast   23

C: Cinderella   39

D: Donkey Prince   55

E: Emperor's New Clothes   69

F: Fisherman and his Wife   81

G: Gingerbread Man   95

H: Humpty Dumpty   107

I: Itsy Bitsy Spider   123

J: Jack and the Beanstalk   135

K: Kings   147

L: Little Mermaid   159

M: Mitten   171

N: Never-Never Land   183

O: Old Lady Who Swallowed a Fly   195

P: Princess and the Pea   205

Q: Queens   217

R: Rapunzel   229

S: Sing a Song of Sixpence   241

T: Thumbelina   253

U: Ugly Duckling   263

V: (Rip) Van Winkle   273

W: Wild Swans   287

X: Fox in Socks   297

Y: Yetta the Trickster   307

Z: Zoos   315

Introduction

Once upon a time, there was a litera-ture-based, ABC-theme book designed to take you through your PreK-1 curricula. This resource helped teachers everywhere, and they all lived happily ever after!

Each of the twenty-six chapters in *Storybook Connections* focuses on one famous fairy tale or storybook linked to a letter of the alphabet, and includes a story summary, art projects, storytime suggestions, math lessons, writing worksheets, vocabulary stretchers, discovery activities, and snacks, plus a selection of games and movement activities. A variety of adorable patterns lend themselves to creative puppet shows, bulletin boards, and more.

Incorporated into the chapters in *Storybook Connections* are important skills and concepts for children to master. Children will work with various creative media (Art), graph a variety of input (Math), explore science and the natural world (Discovery), encounter new and familiar tales (Storytime), and create and enjoy a variety of healthy recipes (Snacks). By interrelating these skills through storybook themes, you will make the activities (and the fairy tales) come alive for every child in your class.

How to Use This Book

Here are some general hints and suggestions to lead you through the sections that appear in each chapter. Of course, your own instincts and experience—as well as your knowledge of the individual children in your classroom—should be your primary guide.

Each chapter in this book begins with a Story Summary. These mini-retellings are primarily for your own use, to familiarize yourself with a story that you may have forgotten. Each chapter also includes a resource list of books to use with the featured tale. Setting the Stage follows. Use these tips and activities to set a festive mood in the classroom. Hang strips of aluminum foil from the doorway so that children can walk "Through the Looking Glass" and into the world of *Alice in Wonderland*, for instance.

 Learning Connection

This section features a writing practice sheet, fancy folder cover (for children to use to store the art from each unit), plus ideas for a vocabulary brainstorming session. Encourage children to help you think of words that begin with the letter you are currently studying. Write the words on the chalkboard as children come up with each one. Help older children look through junior dictionaries to find the meanings of words that are new to them.

 Art

There are usually two or three art activities in each chapter. The materials needed for each project are listed, as well as step-by-step instructions. You can often use the provided patterns in more than one way: to make puppets, flannel board figures, bulletin board decorations, and so on. Provide additional fun materials when available, such as wiggly eyes, glitter, sequins, fabric scraps, and feathers.

 Math

These are whole-class activities that include such skill development areas as estimating, counting, and graphing. You can make a reusable graphing grid by ruling five columns (about two and a half inches wide) onto a piece of butcher paper that is between 60 and 66 inches long. Laminate the finished grid. For each activity, make a copy of the graphing question, color and laminate it, and mount it on the wall above the grid. Make 15 to 20 copies of the category picture symbols found in each section. Use one set as labels for the columns, and give each child a copy of the symbol that represents his or her choice to color and mount in the appropriate column. Use Post-it glue sticks to mount the symbols; they can be easily removed for the next graphing activity.

Discovery

Children are natural scientists—always asking questions and gathering information. The activities in this section provide hands-on opportunities for your class to explore some of the concepts and phenomena associated with the topic in each chapter. We have provided suggestions for water table set-ups, new creations to build at the sand table, and fun ways to observe the great outdoors. You will also find ideas for field trips and in-house speakers.

 ## Games

This section includes a wide variety of movement and card games. Some games are new versions of old favorites, such as "Queen, May I?" and "Pin the Crown on the Donkey." Others let students play adult games with a child's twist, such as "The Queen's Croquet." Dancing is a big part of movement activities, and children can get their whole bodies into the act with "Wonderful Waltzes." They can even pretend to be animals when playing "Adorable Donkeys" and "Side stepping." The stories in this book lend themselves to game- and role-playing. Encourage your students to take these concepts to new levels by adding ideas of their own.

 ## Snacks

Healthy snacks are an important part of every child's day. These treats will be especially popular because they relate to the story that your class is studying. Serve them on special occasions, or have parent volunteers prepare them in class as a cooking project with the children.

Alice's Adventures in Wonderland

STORY SUMMARY

Alice follows a white rabbit down a hole in the ground, only to find herself in . . . Wonderland! In this dream place, she discovers walking and talking playing cards, a cat that can disappear and leave his grin behind, and a queen who is not altogether pleased with Alice's arrival (to put it mildly). Alice is also featured in Lewis Carroll's other classic, *Through the Looking Glass*. Read to your students the first chapter of *Alice's Adventures in Wonderland* from an abridged version for young readers as an introduction to Carroll's fantasy world.

SETTING THE STAGE: CREATING A WONDERLAND

Materials:

Aluminum foil, tape, small paper cups, juice, plastic pitcher, crackers or cookies, tray, blank adhesive labels, marker, stool

Directions:

- Tape sheets of aluminum foil from the top of the door frame. When students enter the classroom, they will step "through the looking glass."
- Near the door, place a tray of paper cups filled with juice and a plastic pitcher labeled "Drink Me." After children drink their juice, tell them to pretend to be like Alice and shrink. Have the children crouch down and pretend to become very small.
- At the other end of the table, place a tray of little cookies or crackers with a label that says "Eat Me." Once the children have taken a few nibbles, let them take turns standing on a stool or going into the doll house corner to give them the sensation of growing taller.

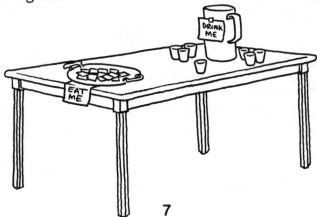

Alice's Adventures in Wonderland
Learning Connection

A IS FOR ALICE . . .

Introduce the students to vocabulary words that begin with "A" that relate to the story, such as Alice, adventure, ask, announce, and arrive. Have the children brainstorm other "amazing A" words that they are already familiar with.

A VERY MERRY UNBIRTHDAY

On a wall calendar, mark each child's birthday. Discuss the meaning of the word "birthday," and that every day of the year that is not a child's birthday is his or her "unbirthday!" Photocopy the year's calendar for each student and help each one to highlight his or her own birthday on it.

ALICE'S WRITING ASSIGNMENT

Duplicate the writing worksheet and give one to each child in the class. Have the children practice printing the letter "A" and words that begin with "A" by copying the examples given.

ALICE'S ADVENTURES FOLDER

Duplicate the folder cover and give one to each child to color and glue to the front of a manila folder. Provide silver watercolors or aluminum foil for children to use to make the looking glass in the center. Children can keep all their work from this unit in their folder.

Alice

apple

A

a

9

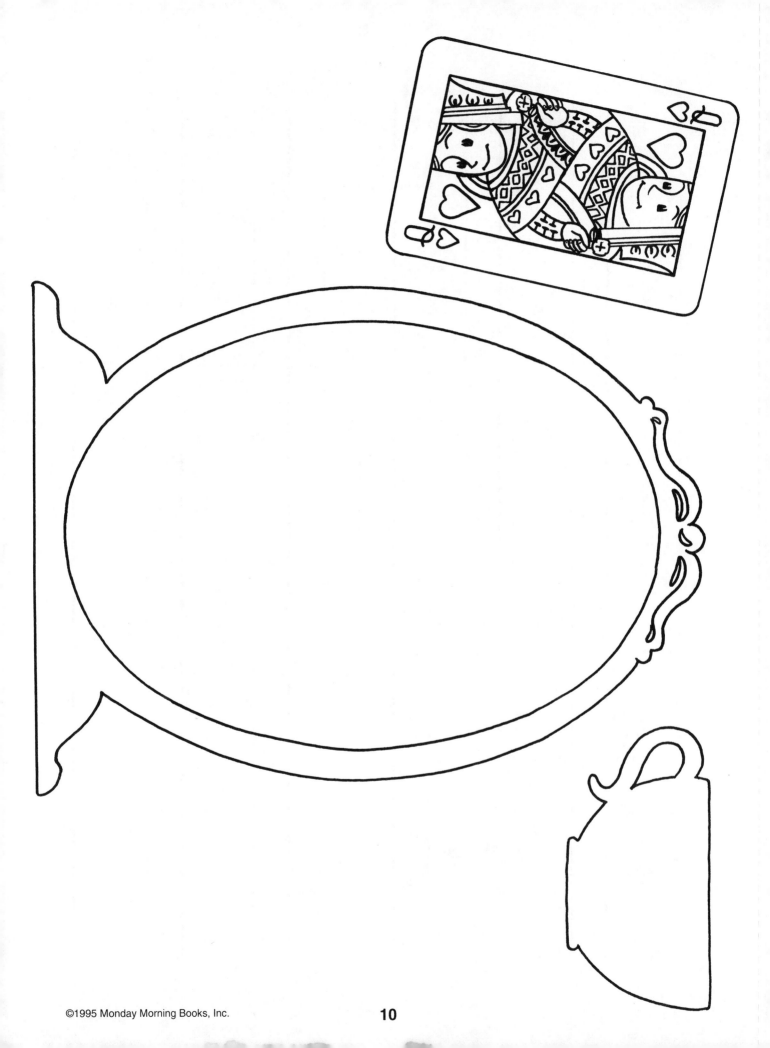

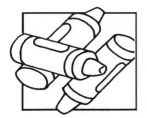

Alice's Adventures in Wonderland
Art Connection

VERY MERRY UNBIRTHDAY CARDS

Materials:
Construction paper, scissors, crayons, nontoxic markers, glitter, glue, used birthday cards (optional)

Directions:
1. Explain that the children will be making "UNbirthday" cards for each other.
2. Let each child choose a piece of colored construction paper.
3. Show the children how to fold the paper in half to make cards. (They can fold it in half twice to make smaller cards.)
4. Have the children decorate these cards to give to their friends. They can cut out pictures from used birthday cards to glue to the cards they make.
5. Help children write messages on the inside of the cards. Let them dictate what they want to say.
6. Designate a time when the children can exchange cards, and have them sing a round of "Happy UNbirthday" to each other.

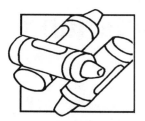

Alice's Adventures in Wonderland
Art Connection

CHESHIRE CAT GRINS

Materials:
Cheshire cat masks, white chalk or crayons, scissors, glue, Popsicle sticks, tagboard

Directions:
1. Enlarge and duplicate the masks onto tagboard and give one to each child.
2. Have the students cut out the grins and color them with white chalk.
3. To play with the masks, the children can hold them up with their hands or glue on Popsicle sticks for handles.
4. Let the children pretend to be Cheshire cats, and disappear behind their wide, happy grins.

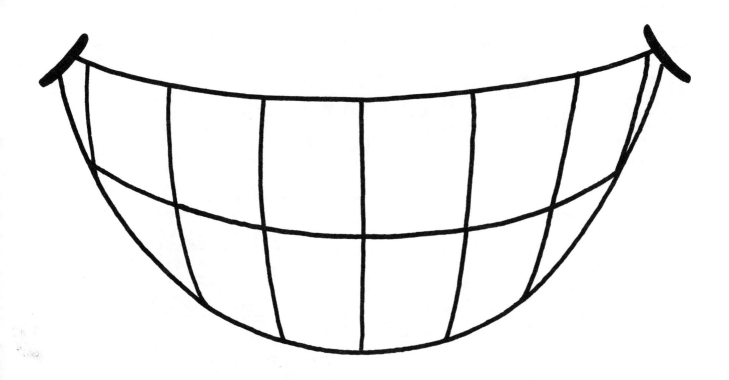

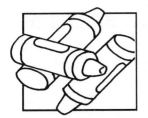

Alice's Adventures in Wonderland
Art Connection

PLAYING CARDS

Materials:
12" x 18" sheets of white construction paper (two per child), hole punch, red yarn, scissors, crayons, markers, deck of cards

Directions:
1. Make "sandwich boards" (see illustration) for the students by punching two holes in the top of each piece of paper, threading a length of red yarn through each set of two holes, and knotting the yarn at the ends to hold.
2. Show the children a deck of real playing cards, and let them examine the numbers, suits, and face cards.
3. Give each child a set of sandwich boards to decorate like playing cards. Let the children use crayons and markers.
4. Gather all of the children together and have them wear their sandwich boards in a "March of the Cards." Allow students to take turns being the Queen and yelling, "Off with their heads!"

Alice's Adventures in Wonderland
Math Connection

WHAT A CARD!

Materials:
Deck of playing cards

Directions:
1. As a class, sort a deck of cards by suits.
2. Remove the face cards.
3. Help the children organize each suit into the correct numerical order, from aces (or "ones") to tens.
4. Have the students mix the cards up and do it again, then play a game of "Go Fish!"

Option 1:
Help children make simple addition and subtraction problems using the cards, for example, ten minus three equals seven.

Option 2:
Have children find different cards that equal the same number. For example, challenge them to find as many ways to make ten as they can—two five cards, a four and a six, a three and a seven, and so on.

Alice's Adventures in Wonderland
Math Connection

I'M LATE!

Materials:
Pocket watch patterns (p. 16), tagboard or oak tag, hole punch, 12" long pieces of yarn, scissors, brads

Directions:
1. Duplicate the watch patterns onto tagboard or oak tag and cut out.
2. Punch two holes in each pattern—one in the center of each watch and another at the top of each watch (as shown).
3. Give each child a watch pattern and a brad and show the children how to insert the brad backwards (with the two "arms" on the front of the watch).
4. Let children string the yarn through the hole at the top of their watches for handles.
5. Help children practice telling time on their watch faces by moving the brad arms. They can pretend to be late for an appointment, just like the White Rabbit!

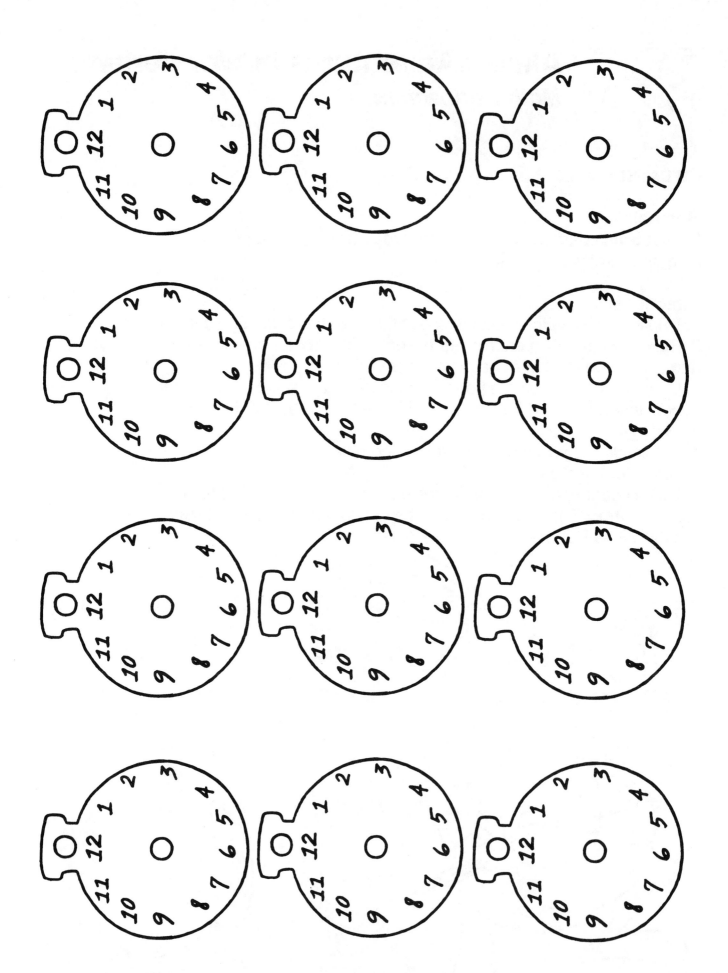

Alice's Adventures in Wonderland
Science Connection

OFF WITH THEIR HEADS!

Materials:
Mirrors (either hand mirrors or free-standing ones)

Directions:
1. Have children look in the mirrors while you talk them through the names of the parts of the head and face.
2. Encourage the children to point to each part as you name it.

Option 1:
If mirrors aren't available, have children pair off and point to the parts of their partner's face while you name them.

Option 2:
Give each child a copy of the Queen's head pattern (p. 18) and a pencil. Have the children write in the names of the parts of the face and head. When they're finished, let them color in their pictures using crayons.

Alice's Adventures in Wonderland
Games Connection

THE QUEEN'S CROQUET

You can play croquet on the lawn, or make an indoor version of the game using cut-out shoe boxes for the wickets. For mallets, purchase plastic yard flamingoes or tape cardboard flamingoes to plastic bats.

DOWN THE RABBIT HOLE

Set up a crawl-through tube in the classroom, or use a playground tube, slide, or tunnel for this activity. Have children take turns being Alice and "falling" down the rabbit's hole. They can slide, wiggle, or squirm through. At the other end, they should pretend to be in Wonderland. As more and more children "arrive" at the other side, they should greet each newcomer who appears through the tunnel.

Note:

This activity is a good way to introduce *Alice's Adventures in Wonderland* to your children. Have each child climb through the tube and then join the group in a circle at the other side. Once all of the class has "arrived," read the tale of Alice and her adventures in Wonderland.

Alice's Adventures in Wonderland
Dramatic Play Connection

MAD HATTER'S TEA PARTY

Let the students take turns playing the roles of the White Rabbit, the Mad Hatter, Alice, the Dormouse, and so on. If possible, provide assorted hats (top hat, sunbonnet, hairband with ears) for children to wear to get in a festive mood.

Materials:

Tea, clear punch cups, milk, sugar cubes, spoons

Directions:

1. Pour cups of tea for the students. (Clear punch cups let the children see the sugar cubes dissolve.)
2. Add milk or sugar for any children who want it. The students love the pouring and stirring, and trying the grown-up drink of tea.

Alice's Adventures in Wonderland
Snack Connection

TEMPTING TARTS

The Queen of Hearts, she baked some tarts,
All on a summer day.
Your children can help bake tarts, too,
*And **eat** them clean away!*

Ingredients:

Pre-made tart shells, cans of cherry pie filling, cookie sheets

Directions:

1. Let children help spoon the cherry pie filling into the shells.
2. Bake the tarts according to the directions on the package.
3. Let the tarts cool, and then serve. (One tart will serve 2-3 children.)

Option:

Make a batch of sugar cookies and let children help cut them out with heart-shaped cutters, then decorate using sprinkles or icing.

Alice's Adventures in Wonderland
Resources

BOOKS

Alice by Whoopi Goldberg, illustrated by John Rocco (Bantam, 1992).
In this creative retelling of *Alice's Adventures . . .* , Wonderland is New York City, and the White Rabbit is an imaginary friend. Alice and two pals travel by subway to pick up a sweepstakes prize.

Alice's Adventures in Wonderland by Lewis Carroll, illustrated by Arthur Rackham (Viking, 1975).
This book has been a joy to audiences since its first publication in 1865. Rackham's paintings and drawings joined the story in 1907.

Alice's Adventures in Wonderland by Lewis Carroll, illustrated by Justin Todd (Crown, 1984).
The illustrator portrays Alice as Alice Liddell, Carroll's original inspiration for the story.

Walt Disney's Alice in Wonderland Meets the White Rabbit by Jane Werner (Golden Press, 1951).
This is an appropriate selection for young children as it features a short text with illustrations from the Disney movie.

OTHER

Newman, Cathy. "The Wonderland of Lewis Carroll." *National Geographic* (June 1991), pp. 100-128.
This informative article tells about Carroll and the history surrounding the creation of "Alice." The feature includes a six-page pull-out poster of numerically ordered illustrations from *Alice's Curious Adventures* and *A Trip Through the Looking Glass*.

Southgate, Ed. *The Queen of Hearts*. Cleveland: Modern Curriculum Press, 1984. Originally, Macmillan, 1982.
This "Purple Star" reader features the poem in an illustrated version with large type for young readers.

Alice in Wonderland (Disney Productions). This videotape is available for purchase or rental at most video stores.

Beauty and the Beast

STORY SUMMARY

Beauty, the youngest of three daughters, asks her father to bring her a rose when he goes away on a trip. Unfortunately, her father picks the flower from a beast's garden, and Beauty must go and live with the beast as punishment. The kind and caring Beauty is able to find goodness in the beast's heart, and falls in love with him. Her kiss breaks a magic spell and returns him to the prince he once was.

SETTING THE STAGE: BUILDING THE BEAST'S CASTLE

Materials:

Mirrors, vase, roses, plastic or wax fangs, garden gloves, glue gun, fake fur, costume jewelry, scarf

Directions:

- Place "magic" mirrors around the classroom for students to view themselves. Have children talk about what they see in the mirrors—their reflections. Then ask them to describe who they are inside (the part of themselves that can't be seen in the mirrors). The book *Mufaro's Beautiful Daughters: An African Tale* by John Steptoe (Lothrop, 1987) addresses the issue of inner and outer beauty.
- Bring a vase of roses into the classroom (remove thorns first). Let the children smell the roses and carefully touch the petals. Option: Use plastic or silk roses and dab a bit of rose water perfume on the petals.
- Provide props for children to use to transform themselves into the Beast or Beauty. For example, plastic or wax fangs can turn any child into a beast, and you can turn garden gloves into beastly paws by attaching fake fur to the backs with a glue gun. (Note: Do not operate a glue gun around children.)

Beauty and the Beast
Learning Connection

B IS FOR BEAUTY . . .
Introduce the students to words that begin with "B," such as big, beast, beauty, beautiful, and brain. Have the children brainstorm as many "B" words as they can.

NATURAL TREASURES
In the story, Beauty's sisters make fun of her for asking her father for a rose instead of for something expensive, such as a fancy gown or a new hat. Ask your students if they think that a flower can be as precious as something bought with money, or if they agree with the sisters. Have them name beautiful objects in nature that they like to observe.

BEAUTY'S WRITING ASSIGNMENT
Duplicate the writing worksheet (p. 25) and give one to each child in the class. Have the children practice printing the letter "B" and words that begin with "B" by copying the examples given or by choosing words from their brainstormed list.

BEAUTY'S FOLDER
Duplicate the folder cover (p. 26) and give one to each child to color and glue to the front of a manila folder. Provide tissue paper for children to glue to the petals, or let them use crayons or watercolors to color the rose. Children can keep all their work from this unit in their folder.

Beauty

beast

B

b

26

Beauty and the Beast
Learning Connection

BEAUTY'S BOOKS

- Plan a field trip to your local library.
- Ask the children to list the books they would want to have in their own library.
- Let children bring their favorite books to school to share.
- Set a literary mood by ordering from the American Library Association (ALA) Disney's Beauty and the Beast poster entitled "Open the Door to Wonder: Get Your Library Card." This poster offers the Disney version of the Beast showing Belle his library. (See Resources for the address of the ALA.)
- Disney's Beauty and the Beast reading diaries, "Letter of Introduction" cards (inviting children to get their library cards), and Beauty and the Beast library card folders are also available from the ALA. (See Resources for details.)
- Disney's Beauty and the Beast Print Kit (see Resources) has a bookmark section.

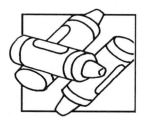

Beauty and the Beast
Art Connection

BEAUTY AND THE BEAST PUPPET SHOW

Students can make their own puppets with these fanciful patterns. Introduce this activity by reading the book *Shadow Play* by Paul Fleischman (Harper and Row, 1990).

Materials:

Puppet patterns (p. 29), scissors, crayons, glitter, glue, sequins, fabric scraps, buttons, Popsicle sticks or straws

Directions:

1. Give each child a set of patterns to color and cut out. Older children may want to use the patterns as stencils to trace and then draw on features.
2. Provide glitter, sequins, fabric scraps, buttons, and other odds and ends for children to use to decorate the patterns.
3. Have the children glue the patterns to Popsicle sticks or straws for handles.
4. Children can put on puppet shows for each other, or they can use the puppets to act out the story as you read or tell it to them.

Option 1:

Provide a large appliance box for children to use for a puppet theater. Cut out a large rectangle in the front and hang paper or fabric curtains.

Option 2:

The children can make bookmarks from the puppet patterns. Reproduce the patterns onto tagboard and let the children color and cut them out.

29

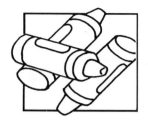

Beauty and the Beast
Art Connection

FANTASY FLOWERS

Children can make a reproduction of the rose that Beauty's father picked, or a bouquet of flowers to give to a friend.

Materials:

Egg carton sections, tissue paper squares, cone-shaped cups, construction paper, scissors, pipe cleaners, straws, Popsicle sticks, tempera paint, paintbrushes, glitter, glue, sequins

Directions:

Show the children how to make three kinds of flowers from the different materials.

- Tissue paper flowers are made by twisting the edges of a square of tissue and then gluing or pasting a pipe cleaner to the base.
- Egg carton cups (individual sections) can be painted and decorated with colored glitter and sequins. Glue on straws, Popsicle sticks, or pipe cleaners for stems.
- Cone-shaped cups can be decorated with paints and glitter. Have the children wrap the top of a pipe cleaner around the bottom of the cone and glue in place for a stem.

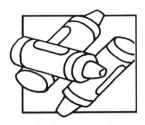

Beauty and the Beast
Art Connection

MAGIC MIRRORS

Tell the students that they are going to make "magic" mirrors that will let them see anything or anyone in the world!

Materials:

Mirror patterns (p. 32), tagboard, scissors, crayons, old magazines, glitter, glue, paper

Directions:

1. Duplicate enough mirror patterns onto tagboard for every child in the class to have one.
2. Provide magazines for children to use to cut out pictures of objects, places, or people they find appealing. They can glue these to the round part of the magic mirror. Children can also draw their own pictures onto round pieces of paper to glue to their magic mirror.
3. Let children decorate the handle and border of their mirrors using crayons, glitter, and glue.

Option:

Take Polaroid photographs of children and let them glue these to the round part of the mirror pattern. Extend this activity by having children tell you one thing they like about themselves. Write their responses on 3" x 5" index cards to place under each child's mirror. Display the mirrors and cards on the classroom bulletin board.

Beauty and the Beast
Math Connection

A ROSE IS A ROSE IS A ROSE

In this story, Beauty requests that her father bring her a rose from his travels. See if your students also prefer a rose to other flowers.

Materials:

Flower patterns (p. 34), scissors, crayons, large piece of construction paper, glue

Directions:

1. Duplicate the flower patterns and make a five-column chart, gluing one flower to the top of each column.
2. Write the name of each flower beneath the pattern.
3. Ask the children to choose which flower they like best.
4. Graph and discuss the responses with the children.

Option 1:

Photocopy additional flower patterns for children to glue in the columns as markers.

Option 2:

Bring in real flowers for the children to observe and smell.

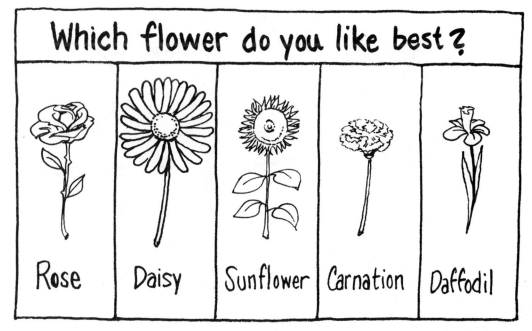

Which flower do you like best?

| Rose | Daisy | Sunflower | Carnation | Daffodil |

Which flower do you you like best?

34

Beauty and the Beast
Discovery Connection

MIRROR MARVELS

Materials:
Mirrors

Directions:
1. Place mirrors opposite each other.
2. Have the children take turns standing between the mirrors so that they can see their reflections both in front and behind.
3. Let children place a variety of objects between the mirrors and view the reflections and re-reflections.

Option:
Have reflection relays. Post a target on the wall (such as a picture of Beauty and the Beast) and have students bounce the beam from a strong flashlight off three or four mirrors until it hits the target.

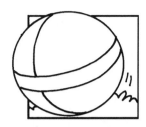

Beauty and the Beast
Games Connection

BEING BEASTLY!

Have your students imagine that they are beasts. They can begin by growling and stretching their arms toward the ceiling to appear larger. Then have them stomp in place, lifting their feet high and setting them back down heavily. Let the children line up, and have them stomp and growl in a row, following a beastly leader. (The leader could wear beast paws; see p. 23.)

BEASTLY TAG

Designate one child to be the beast. Have the rest of the children line up against a wall (or, if this game is played outside, along a fence). All of the children run across the room or yard and try to touch the opposite wall before the beast tags them. Those who are caught become "beasts," too, and help the original beast tag other children. Play continues until all children have been caught, and the last one tagged is the first beast in the next game.

Beauty and the Beast
Snack Connection

BEASTLY BREAD

Beastly Bread is monstrously fun to make!

Ingredients:

Milk, white bread, food coloring, new inexpensive paintbrushes, small plastic bowls

Directions:

1. Divide 1/3 cup of milk among several small bowls.
2. Add enough food coloring to turn the milk a vibrant color.
3. Give each student a new paintbrush to use to decorate a plain slice of bread with the milk-paint.
4. When the children have finished drawing designs on the bread, toast the pieces of bread in a toaster oven. Toasting will highlight the children's artwork.

Option:

Talk about table manners and good etiquette. Play "Be Our Guest" from the Disney soundtrack to *Beauty and the Beast* (Walt Disney Records, 1991).

Beauty and the Beast
Resources

BOOKS

Beauties and Beasts collected by Betsy Hearne, illustrated by Joanne Caroselli (Oryx, 1993). This extensive collection of stories from around the world is accompanied by fascinating background material, activities, and sources for additional reading. It includes several versions of "Beauty and the Beast" and "Cupid and Psyche."

Beauty and the Beast retold and illustrated by Warwick Hutton (Atheneum, 1985). Watercolor paintings alternate with full pages of text. A kind and beautiful maid releases a handsome prince from his beastly spell.

Beauty and the Beast retold by Marianna Mayer, illustrated by Mercer Mayer (Four Winds Press, 1978). Full pages of text alternate with large, elaborately detailed illustrations.

Mufaro's Beautiful Daughters: An African Tale by John Steptoe (Lothrop, 1987). This Caldecott Honor Book tells the tale of two sisters, one with inner beauty and the other with outer beauty. Which one will overcome events to become the queen?

Shadow Play by Paul Fleischman, pictures by Eric Beddows (Harper and Row, 1990). In this variation, a brother and sister are enchanted by a shadow play presentation at a country fair of "Beauty and the Beast" in which all of the shadows are made by one man. Outstanding black and white illustrations with intricate detail tell this story in a unique way.

Sleeping Beauty and Other Favourite Tales by Angela Carter, illustrated by Michael Foreman (Otter Books, 1991). The English translation of the version by Madame Leprince de Beaumont of Beauty and the Beast is found on pages 45-62. Many black and white illustrations, also full-color illustrations with at least four full-page illustrations.

OTHER

Beauty and the Beast read by Peter Bartlett, Eira Heath, and Anna Barry (Durkin Hayes, 1994). This cassette is in the paperback audio classic tale series.

Beauty and the Beast (Playhouse, 1986). This is the sixth volume in the Faerie Tale Theatre series.

Beauty and the Beast: The Original Motion Picture Soundtrack (Walt Disney Records, 1991). Music by Alan Menken, lyrics by Howard Ashman.

"Classroom Connections: Taming the Beast," *Booklinks*, Vol. 1, #3 pp. 34-39. The article, written by Ann Welton, explains how to use fairy tales to introduce social issues and includes bibliographies on "Beauty and the Beast," "War," "Immigration: Prejudice and Acceptance," and "The Environment."

Disney's Beauty and the Beast Print Kit
Disney Computer Software
500 S. Buena Vista Street
Burbank, CA 91521

American Library Association
50 E. Huron Street
Chicago, IL 60611
   • Disney's Beauty and the Beast poster (order #982; $5.00)
   • Disney's Beauty and the Beast reading diaries (order #984; 100 for $4.00)
   • Belle's "Letter of Introduction" (order #986; 200 for $4.00)
   • Disney's Beauty and the Beast library card folders (order #983; 50 for $8.00)

Cinderella

STORY SUMMARY

Cinderella works from dawn until dusk for her lazy stepmother and two stepsisters. When they forbid her to go to a ball at the palace, her fairy godmother appears and uses magic to help her. Cinderella attends the ball in disguise, with the reminder to be home by midnight, when the magic will wear off. She meets the prince, but leaves him at the stroke of twelve. He searches everywhere for her, and finally locates her—much to the surprise of her evil family—with the help of her lost slipper.

SETTING THE STAGE: CINDERELLA'S CINDERS

Materials:

Sponges, bucket, scrub brush, mop, soapy water, slipper, paper crown, wand, waltz music, streamers

Directions:

- Provide simple props for students to use when acting out the story. Equip your "home center" with cleaning supplies. Let children help clean up after snack, using sponges and soapy water, cloth towels, or brooms.
- Place party clothes as well as ragged clothes in the dress-up corner. Set out a wand (for a fairy godmother), a special slipper, and a paper crown.
- Provide crepe paper streamers for children to use to transform a corner into a castle ballroom. Set up a tape player or stereo system nearby, and play waltz music for the children to dance to.

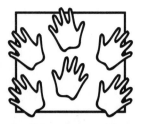

Cinderella
Learning Connection

C IS FOR CINDERELLA . . .
Introduce the students to words that begin with "C," such as cinder, castle, carriage, clock, and coach. Emphasize all of the words that begin with the hard "C" sound ("coach") and the soft "C" sound ("cinder"). Have the children brainstorm as many "C" words as they can.

BREAKING THE STEREOTYPE
Discuss different types of families. Ask questions that relate to the story, such as, "Are stepmothers as evil as they're shown to be in fairy tales?" "Why do you think that the tale was written that way?" "How else could the story be told?"

CINDERELLA'S WRITING ASSIGNMENT
Duplicate the writing worksheet (p. 41) and give one to each child in the class. Have the children practice printing the letter "C" and words that begin with "C" by copying the examples given or choosing words from the brainstormed list.

CINDERELLA'S FOLDER
Duplicate the folder cover (p. 42) and give one to each child to color and glue to the front of a manila folder. Provide gold glitter for children to sprinkle and glue to the slipper to make it sparkle. Children can keep all their work from this unit in their folder.

Cinderella

coach

C

c

41

42

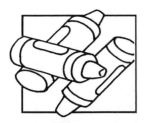

Cinderella
Art Connection

CINDER-ARTISTS

Materials:
Cinderella-in-rags patterns (one per child; p. 44), red construction paper, charcoal pencils, scissors, glue

Directions:
1. Have students draw on red paper (bricks) with charcoal pencils or sticks to create "ash" pictures.
2. Let the children color and cut out the Cinderella patterns and glue to the red paper.
3. Post the completed pictures on a "Cinder-Artists" bulletin board.

Option 1:
Use red brick corrugated paper to cover the bulletin board.

Option 2:
Provide pieces of uncooked spaghetti for children to glue to Cinderella's broom for a three-dimensional appearance.

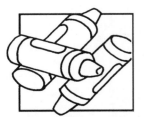

Cinderella
Art Connection

CINDERELLAS AND THEIR FELLAS

Materials:
Butcher paper, crayons, scissors, fishing wire, clothespins

Directions:
1. Have the "ellas" and the "fellas" lay down on butcher paper.
2. Trace around each child, and have the children cut out their paper selves.
3. On one side of the paper, the children can draw themselves in rags. On the other side, they can draw appropriate dress for a fancy ball.
4. Suspend the paper children with clothespins from fishing wire strung across the classroom.

BEFORE AND AFTER
This is a smaller-scale version of "Cinderellas and their Fellas."

Materials:
White drawing paper, crayons, markers

Directions:
1. Give each child a sheet of white drawing paper to fold in half.
2. On one side of the paper, have the children draw pictures of themselves in their favorite worn-out clothes.
3. On the other side of the paper, have the children draw pictures of themselves in their fanciest dress-up outfits.
4. Post the completed pictures on a "Before and After" bulletin board.

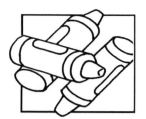

Cinderella
Art Connection

TWINKLE TOES

Materials:
Butcher paper, scissors, plastic tarps or old shower curtains, two dishpans or small tubs, silver tempera paint, soapy water, towels, high-heeled shoe

Directions:
1. With the help of an art room assistant or parent volunteer, put down strips of butcher paper on plastic tarps or old shower curtains.
2. Cover the bottom of a dishpan or small tub with silver tempera paint.
3. Have the students take off their shoes, then put on one high heel. Have them step into the paint with both the shod and the unshod foot and walk across the paper.
4. At the other end of the paper, have another adult and a tub of water and plenty of towels for cleaning the painted feet.

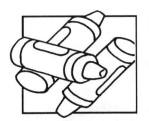

Cinderella
Art Connection

PUMPKIN CARRIAGE

Materials:
Coach pattern (p. 48), orange construction or butcher paper, scissors, pie tin, gold tempera paint, glue, dish-washing sponges

Directions:
1. Cut out large pumpkin shapes (one per child) from the orange paper, using the coach pattern as a stencil.
2. Duplicate the coach patterns (one per child).
3. Have the children glue their coach pattern to one side of the pumpkin.
4. Set out gold paint in pie tins and dish-washing sponges with a wand-like handle (see illustration) for children to share.
5. Let the students take turns dipping the sponges in the gold paint, tapping the pumpkin in one or two places, and magically turning it into a coach (by turning the paper over).
6. After the papers dry, let children decorate the coach side of the paper.

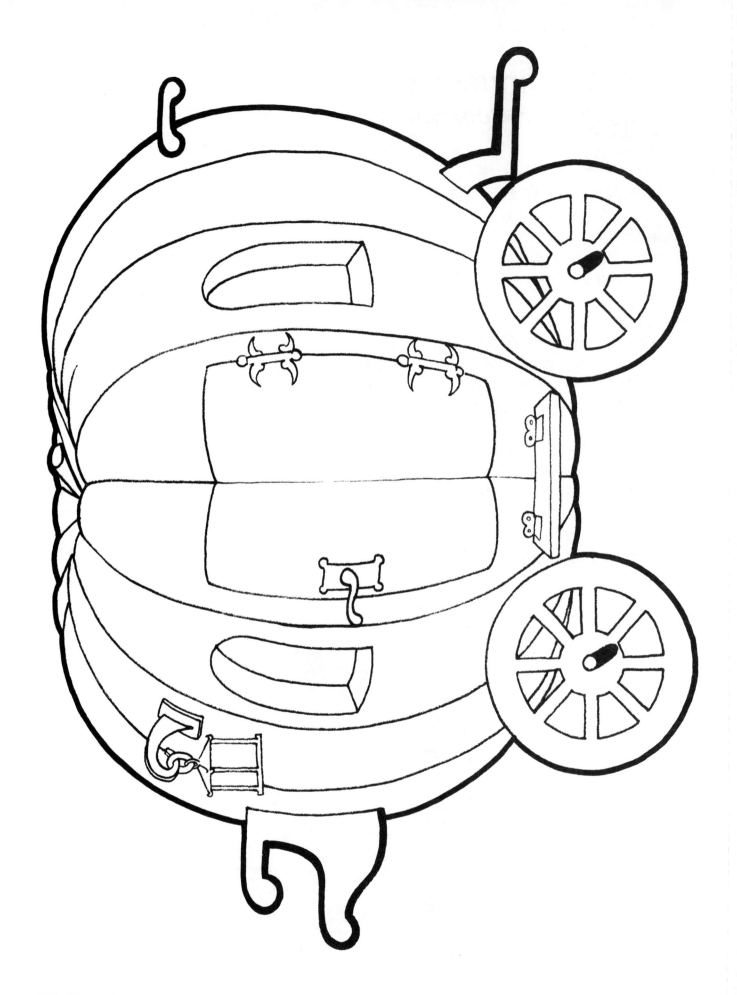

48

Cinderella
Math Connection

CLOCK FACES

Draw attention to a clock in the room. Focus on the part of Cinderella in which her fairy godmother tells Cinderella she must return by midnight.

Materials:
Clocks

Directions:
1. Set the clock faces to reflect midnight.
2. Help the children read the clocks, noting that both noon and midnight occur when the big hand and the little hand point at twelve.
3. Reset the clock to show a few minutes before twelve. Have the children run from the room at the stroke of twelve, and go to the next activity.

Note: If possible, bring in a digital clock and a clock that tolls on the hour.

Option:
Provide pictures of various sized clocks for children to observe. Cut ads for wristwatches from magazines, and have children compare them to pictures of Big Ben (or other large clocks).

Cinderella
Math Connection

SUPER SLIPPERS!

Materials:
Shoe patterns, scissors, crayons, paste, large sheet of paper (for graph)

Directions:
1. Make a shoe graph and glue one of the shoe patterns to the top of each column.
2. Ask children to look at their shoes and then to pick a pattern that best matches the shoes they are wearing.
3. Let children color the patterns to look like their shoes.
4. Have the children take turns pasting their shoe pattern into the appropriate column.
5. Help children read the results of the graph. Ask them questions such as, "How many people are wearing sneakers today?" "How many people are wearing sandals?" You can take this activity further by dividing the graphing by colors.

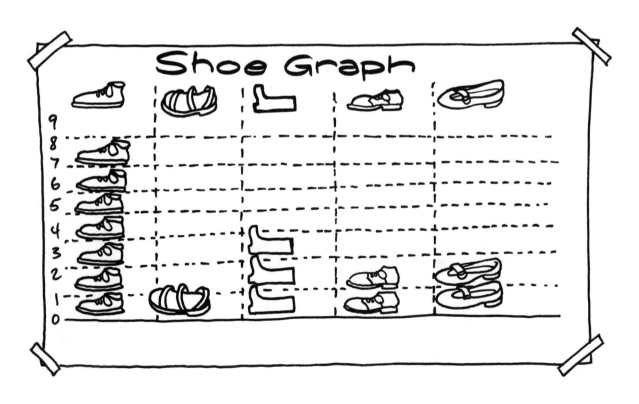

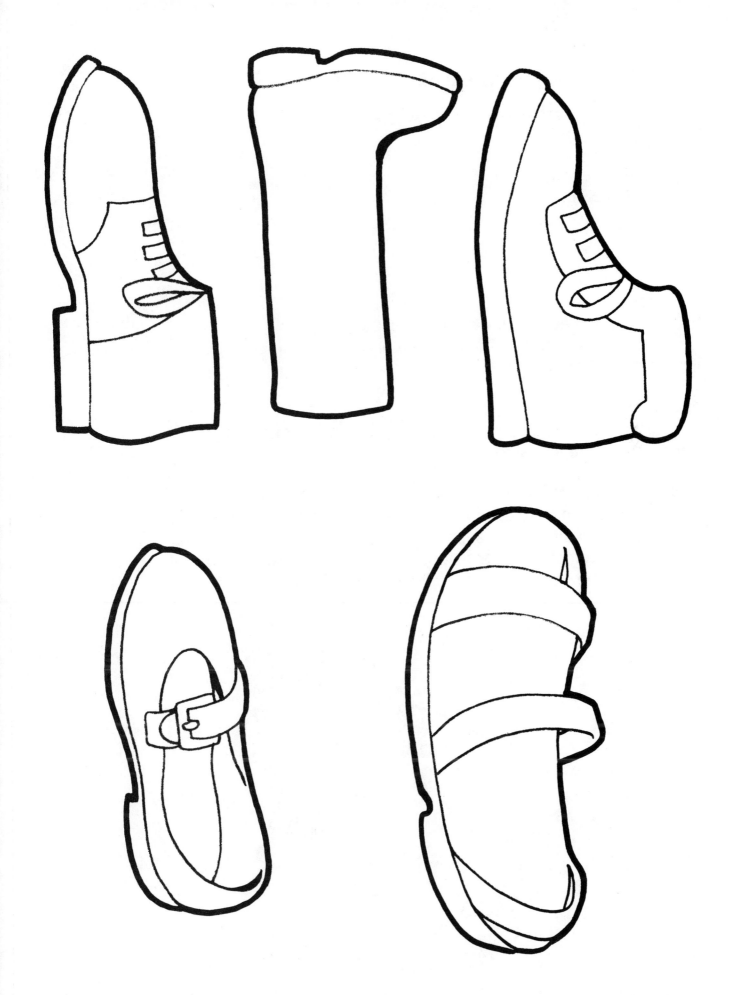

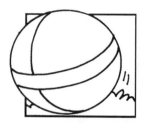

Cinderella
Games Connection

WHOSE SHOE?

Materials:
Children's shoes

Directions:
1. Collect one of each of the students' shoes.
2. Hide the shoes around the play area and have each student try to find his or her missing shoe.

Option:
You can play this as a detective game, with one student trying to match each shoe to a student.

WONDERFUL WALTZES
After students have shoes on both feet again, let them practice waltzing to classical waltz music, such as "The Blue Danube Waltz." You can also put on rock 'n roll or other fun music for children to really swing to. Or show children dance steps to practice in pairs.

Cinderella
Snack Connection

CASTLE CUPCAKES

Ingredients:
Cupcake mix, whipped topping, food coloring, decorating materials (pillow candies, chocolate bars, sugar cones, toothpicks, tape, paper, scissors)

Directions:
1. Follow the instructions on your favorite cupcake mix or recipe and make a batch of cupcakes.
2. When the cupcakes have cooled, students can frost them with whipped topping tinted with a few drops of food coloring. Children can choose from the following ways to decorate their cupcake castles:
- pillow candies work for battlements along the top edges
- two or four segments from a chocolate bar and a couple of colored toothpicks make a fun yet simple drawbridge
- sugar cones can be inverted to make turrets on top of the cupcakes
- small pieces of paper and a toothpick with tape make tiny flags for the castles

Cinderella
Resources

BOOKS

Cinderella by Mimi Everett (Sunbird Publishing, 1990).
This small book features picture-match words on each double set of pages.

Cinderella by the Grimm Brothers, retold and illustrated by Nonny Hogrogian (Greenwillow, 1981).
In this well-researched version, full-page illustrations alternate with pages of very small print text.

Cinderella by Barbara Karlin, illustrated by James Marshall (Little, Brown, 1989).
James Marshall's classic illustrations accompany the famous story. Cinderella hastily tries to flee the palace before the fairy godmother's magic loses effect, and leaves a glass slipper behind.

Cinderella by Charles Perrault, translated and illustrated by Diane Goode (Knopf, 1988).
In this traditional version, a mistreated kitchen maid attends the palace ball with the help of her fairy godmother.

Cinderella by Eulalia Valeri (Silver Burdett, 1981).
This wordless version (with short text on the back cover) is perfect to assist young students in dictating their own versions of the story.

The Cinderella Rebus Book by Ann Morris, illustrated by Ljilianna Rylands (Orchard Books, 1989).
A combination of text and rebus illustrations helps the beginning reader to tell this tale.

The Egyptian Cinderella by Shirley Climo, illustrated by Ruth Heller (Crowell, 1989).
Beautiful color illustrations help to tell this story from another culture's perspective.

In the Land of Small Dragon by Dang Mahn Kha (Viking Press, 1979).
In this Vietnamese folk tale, a dutiful daughter, mistreated by her stepmother, is rewarded by her fairy godmother.

Prince Cinders by Babette Cole (Putnam's, 1987).
This silly story is a modern turn on the Cinderella fable. A fairy grants a small, skinny prince a change in appearance and the chance to go to the Palace Disco. Short text and lively illustrations make this version a hit with youngsters.

Princess Furball by Charlotte Huck (Greenwillow, 1989).
In this variation of Cinderella, a princess in a coat of a thousand furs hides her identity from a king who falls in love with her. Colorful and detailed illustrations accompany the text.

Sidney Rella and the Glass Sneaker by Bernice Myers (Macmillan, 1985).
Sidney Rella becomes a football player with a little help from his fairy godfather.

Walt Disney's Cinderella and Her Animal Friends: A Book About Kindness (Golden Books, 1987).
From Disney's Classic Value Tales series, this adaptation uses illustrations from the film and short text to make a social skills point. Available in hard- and soft-cover editions.

Yeh-Shen: A Cinderella Story from China by Ai-Ling Louie (Philomel Books, 1982).
This story features historically researched illustrations. A young girl overcomes the wickedness of her stepsister and stepmother to become the bride of a prince. Based on an ancient Chinese manuscript.

OTHER

Cinderella (CBS Video, 1984).
This video stars Jennifer Beals, Matthew Broderick, Jean Stapleton, and Eve Arden.

 # Donkey Prince

STORY SUMMARY

A childless king and queen ask a wizard for assistance in conceiving a child. However, when the greedy king tries to cheat the wizard out of full payment, the wizard casts a spell upon the baby. The infant prince is born in the form of a donkey. Although their young son is blessed with a wonderful musical talent, the king and queen cannot see beyond his donkey skin. The true love of a wise princess breaks the wizard's spell.

SETTING THE STAGE: DECORATING FOR DONKEYS

Materials:

Stringed instruments (lute, ukulele, guitar, violin, cello) and recordings of music from the same instruments (see Resources for lute music recordings; p. 68), gray cape, donkey-ear headbands (p. 59), "royal" dress-up clothes, mirror

Directions:

- Display a variety of stringed instruments on a low table in the music center. Let the children take turns holding the instruments.
- Play recordings of string music.
- Put a gray cape in the dress-up center for children to wear when pretending to be The Donkey Prince. Add paper ears glued to a headband for a more realistic costume. The child wearing the donkey costume can easily shed his or her "skin" when retelling this tale.
- The queen in this story likes to try on fancy clothes and admire herself in mirrors. Place an assortment of fancy clothes in the dress-up area, and position a mirror nearby.

The Donkey Prince
Learning Connection

D IS FOR DONKEY . . .
Introduce the students to words that start with "D," such as donkey, desire, delightful, and door. Have the students brainstorm as many "D" words as they can.

EEYORE IS A DEPRESSED DONKEY
Discuss another famous donkey that the children might know: Eeyore. Read the children a story about Eeyore, such as "Eeyore Has a Birthday and Gets Two Presents" in *Winnie-the-Pooh* by A. A. Milne, illustrated by Ernest Shepard, colored by Hilda Scott (Dutton, 1974).

DONKEY'S WRITING ASSIGNMENT
Duplicate the writing worksheet (p. 57) and give one to each child in the class. Have the children practice printing the letter "D" and words that begin with "D" by copying the examples given.

DONKEY'S FOLDER
Duplicate the folder cover (p. 58) onto gray paper and give a copy to each child to decorate and glue to the front of a manila folder. Children can cut crowns from yellow construction paper to glue to the top of their folders. Or let them sprinkle gold glitter on top of white construction paper crowns. Children can keep all the work from this unit in their folder.

Donkey

dance

D

d

58

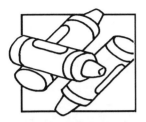

The Donkey Prince
Art Connection

DONKEY EARS

Materials:
Gray and pink construction paper, gray construction paper strips (1" x 18") tagboard or oak tag, scissors, tape, stapler, glue

Directions:
1. Duplicate triangles onto oak tag or tagboard and cut out to make templates.
2. Let children use the triangle patterns to cut out gray triangles and pink triangles.
3. Have children glue the pink triangles onto the gray triangles to make the donkey ears.
4. Make headbands from the construction paper strips by fitting the strips around each child's head to measure, and then cutting off the excess paper and stapling the ends together.
5. Show children how to glue the ears to the headbands.

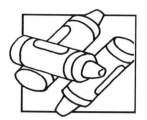

The Donkey Prince
Art Connection

THE PERSON WITHIN

Materials:
Donkey patterns (p. 61), crayons, scissors

Directions:
1. Discuss the fact that surface appearances can be deceiving. For instance, the king and queen in this story couldn't see beyond their son's donkey fur to the warm and talented human within.
2. Have the children think about both their differences and similarities, and tell them that they are each unique and special, both inside and out.
3. Give the children donkey patterns and have them use crayons to draw their own faces in the empty circle.
4. Encourage children to think about their different talents. Help them brainstorm the things they like to do and the qualities that they appreciate about themselves. Then have the children add symbols for these talents and activities to their picture. (The Donkey Prince could play the lute and sing beautiful songs. Your students might be great at baseball, piano, being a sister or brother, and so on.)
5. Post their completed pictures on a "Delightful Donkeys" bulletin board.

Option:
Take pictures of your students and let them cut out their faces and glue them to the circle in the donkey patterns.

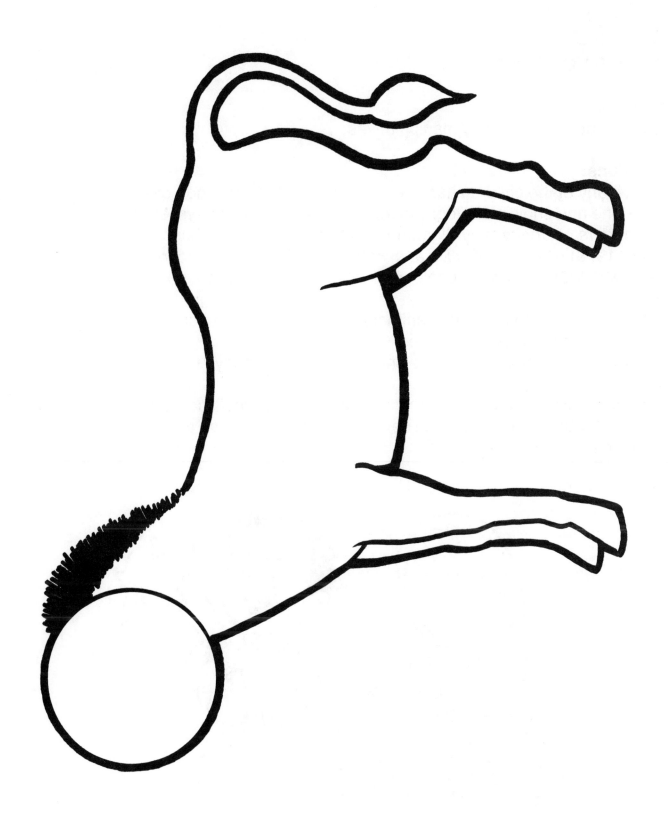

The Donkey Prince
Discovery Connection

DISCUSSING DONKEYS

Materials:
Books on donkeys, donkey manipulatives

Directions:
1. Ask if any of the children has ever seen a real donkey. If not, describe one and show a photograph from a book about donkeys, such as *Wonders of Donkeys* by Sigmund A. Lavine and Vincent Scuro (Dodd, 1978). *What Do You Do at a Petting Zoo?* by Hana Machotka (Morrow, 1990) has a color photograph of two donkeys and a page of facts.
2. Ask if the children can name animals that look similar to donkeys, for example, horses, ponies, mules.
3. Have the children make the braying sounds of a donkey, "Hee-haw! Hee-haw!"
4. Many toy stores and teacher resource stores carry realistic plastic animals. Try to find a donkey and several horses for children to examine in the manipulatives area.

The Donkey Prince
Math Connection

COUNTING COINS

In this story, The Donkey Prince's father (the king) enjoys counting his money—silver and gold coins and bars. Your students can practice their counting skills with faux riches.

Materials:

Coin and bar patterns (p. 64), silver and gold paper (you can substitute gray for silver and yellow for gold), scissors, paper crowns

Directions:

1. Duplicate the bar patterns onto silver or gray paper and cut out.
2. Duplicate the coin patterns onto gold or yellow paper and cut out.
3. Place the coins and bars on a low table.
4. Let children take turns playing royalty counting their money. They can wear paper crowns while counting.

Option:

Use poker chips sprayed with gold paint for coins that children can stack, and small cardboard boxes covered with aluminum foil or gold Contact paper for bars.

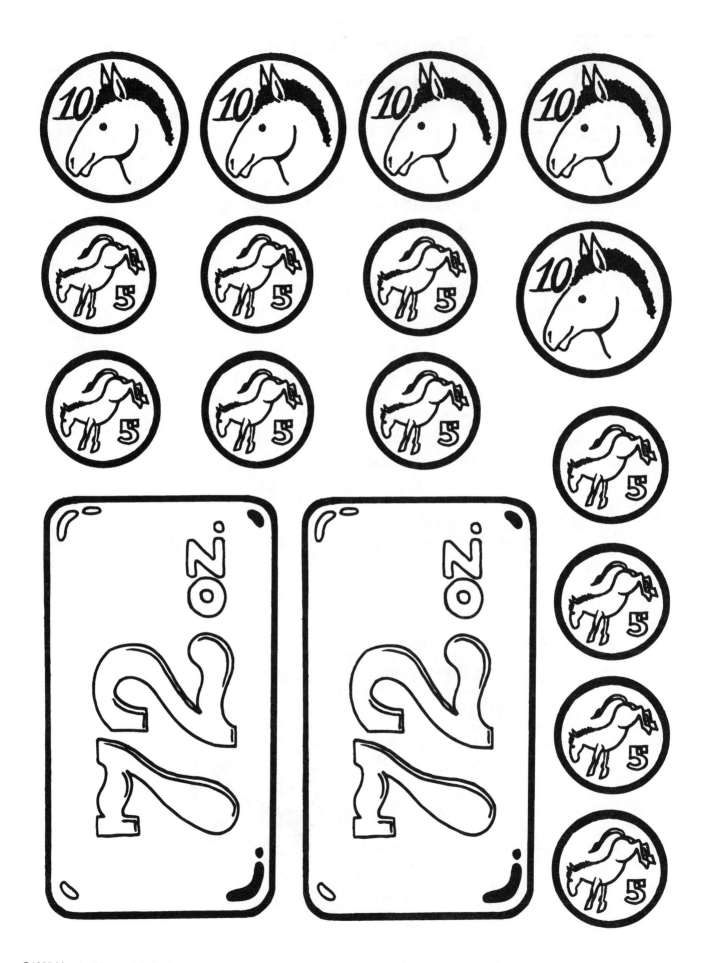

The Donkey Prince
Games Connection

ADORABLE DONKEYS

Materials:
Donkey-ear headbands (p. 59)

Directions:
1. Have your students put on their donkey-ear headbands and then line up in a row.
2. Let them warm up by counting horse-fashion, stomping one foot on the ground as you call out numbers to them.
3. Explain that they are going to practice donkey kicks, and either describe or demonstrate one.
4. Once children have gotten the hang of donkey-kicking, hold a game of kickball. (The prince in M. Jean Craig's version of this story is very good at this game.)

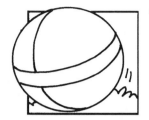

The Donkey Prince
Games Connection

PIN THE CROWN ON THE DONKEY

Materials:
Donkey head pattern from folder cover (p. 58), crown pattern, scissors, double-stick tape, cloth blindfold

Directions:
1. Enlarge the donkey head pattern.
2. Duplicate the crown pattern at the bottom of this page, cut out, and back with double-stick tape.
3. Play this game as you would play "Pin the Tail on the Donkey," except that the children should try to place the crown on the Donkey Prince's head.

Note: Students who do not wish to be blindfolded may shut their eyes instead.

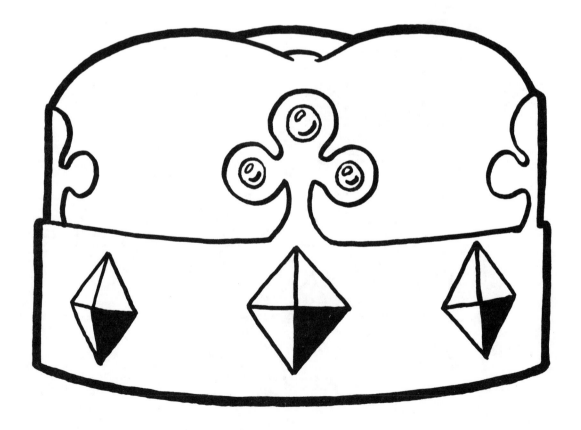

The Donkey Prince
Snack Connection

CARROT COINS

Ingredients:
Carrots, knife

Directions:
1. Cut the carrots into circles (medallions).
2. Let the children stack their carrot coins and count them—just like the king in the story.
3. Have the children gobble up their "gold."

Option:
Provide a variety of dipping sauces for children to eat with their carrot coins.

The Donkey Prince
Resources

BOOKS

Donkey Prince by M. Jean Craig, illustrated by Barbara Cooney (Doubleday, 1977).
This version tells the tale of a donkey-child who sheds his skin when he meets with true love.

Francisco by Robert Maiorano (Macmillan, 1978).
A young boy in the Dominican Republic must provide food for his family while his father is away. This is a very good story about problem solving.

The King at the Door by Brock Cole (Doubleday, 1979).
A king pays a visit to a local inn, but only a young boy believes that he is really a king, and is rewarded. The short text alternates with black and white and color illustrations.

Sleeping Beauty and Other Favourite Fairy Tales, chosen and translated by Angela Carter (Schocken, 1984).
The English translation of Charles Perrault's version of "Donkey-skin" is included in this wonderful resource. Black and white sketches alternate with three full-color illustrations.

Wales' Tale by Susan Saunders (Viking Press, 1980).
Because Sara has a kind face, Wales (a talking donkey who claims he is an enchanted prince) asks for help in breaking the spell. This story is complete with a surprise ending!

Winnie-the-Pooh by A. A. Milne, illustrated by Ernest Shepard, colored by Hilda Scott (Dutton, 1974).
Read the children a chapter of this book at a time, showing the beautifully colored pictures.

Wonders of Donkeys by Sigmund A. Lavine & Vincent Scuro (Dodd, 1978).
This non-fiction book is filled with information on donkeys. Black and white pictures accompany the text.

OTHER

Amarilli, Mia Bella (Harmonia Mundi France, 1985).
This is a recording of Rene Jacobs and Konrad Junghanel in concert.

Amours de P. de Ronsard (selections) (Harmonia Mundi France, 1985).
These recordings are from music by de Bertrand (ca. 1581).

Winnie-the-Pooh and a Day for Eeyore (Walt Disney Home Video, 1983).
This videotape emphasizes the value of being kind and thoughtful in social relationships.

Emperor's New Clothes

STORY SUMMARY

Two traveling tricksters swindle the Emperor by appealing to his vanity. The con artists use smooth talk to convince the Emperor that they make the best cloth in the world. They claim that only the smartest people are able to actually see the cloth. The tricksters (and the Emperor) are exposed by a little boy who calls things as he sees them!

SETTING THE STAGE: THE EMPEROR'S CLOSET

Materials:

Dressing dolls, lacing cards, button books, spools of thread, plastic hangers for children's clothes, mirrors, bathrobes, paper crowns

Directions:

- Set up a sewing-corner display with dressing dolls, lacing cards, and button books. Collect spools of colored thread for children to stack and examine.
- This unit provides the perfect opportunity for children to practice self-help skills. Show them how to zip zippers, tie shoelaces, use Velcro, and pull on boots.
- Encourage children to practice hanging clothes on plastic hangers. (Parents will be impressed when their children begin hanging up their clothes at home!)
- Set up mirrors in the dress-up area. Provide a few "royal" robes (bathrobes) for children to wear. Place paper crowns nearby. Children can try on the robes and crowns and admire their royal selves in the mirrors.

The Emperor's New Clothes
Learning Connection

E IS FOR EMPEROR . . .

Introduce the students to words that begin with "E," such as emperor, embarrassed, excited, envy, everyone, and empty. Have the children brainstorm as many "E" words as they can.

SEW-AND-SEW

Cut oversized needles from thin cardboard and cover them with gold or silver Contact paper. Attach lengths of thick yarn and let students weave their own "cloth" around chair and table legs.

THE EMPEROR'S WRITING ASSIGNMENT

Duplicate the writing worksheet (p. 71) and give one to each child in the class. Have the children practice printing the letter "E" and words that begin with "E" by copying the examples given. They can also write words from their excellent brainstorming lists.

EMPEROR'S FOLDER

Duplicate the folder cover (p. 72) and give one to each child to color and glue to the front of a manila folder. Give children copies of the Emperor's clothes patterns (p. 74) to color, cut out, and glue to their closet folder cover. Children can keep all the work from this unit in their folder.

Emperor

excited

E

e

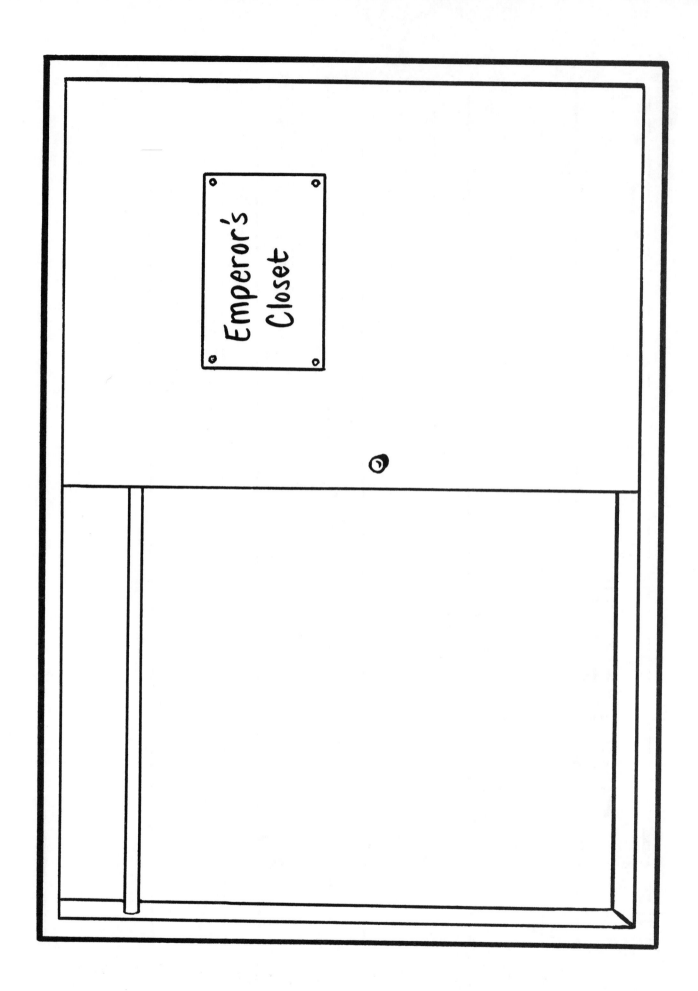

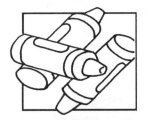

The Emperor's New Clothes
Art Connection

THE EMPEROR AND HIS CLOTHES
Encourage children to play at being clothes designers and create real clothes for the gullible Emperor.

Materials:
Emperor and clothes patterns (one per child; p. 74), scissors, construction paper, oak tag or tagboard, crayons, paper clips

Directions:
1. Duplicate the Emperor patterns onto oak tag or tagboard and cut out.
2. Copy the clothes patterns for each child to color and cut out. (Note: Depending on the motor control of your group, either have students cut the patterns out themselves or cut the patterns out ahead of time.) Older children can use the outlines of the clothes as templates, and cut out their own construction paper clothes for their Emperors.
3. Let children decorate clothes for the Emperor dolls. They can make the clothes stay on with paper clips.

Option:
Make a flannel board using these patterns to retell the story. Cut out the patterns and glue a small piece of felt to the back of the Emperor and his clothes. Keep the Emperor in his boxers for the finale.

73 ©1995 Monday Morning Books, Inc.

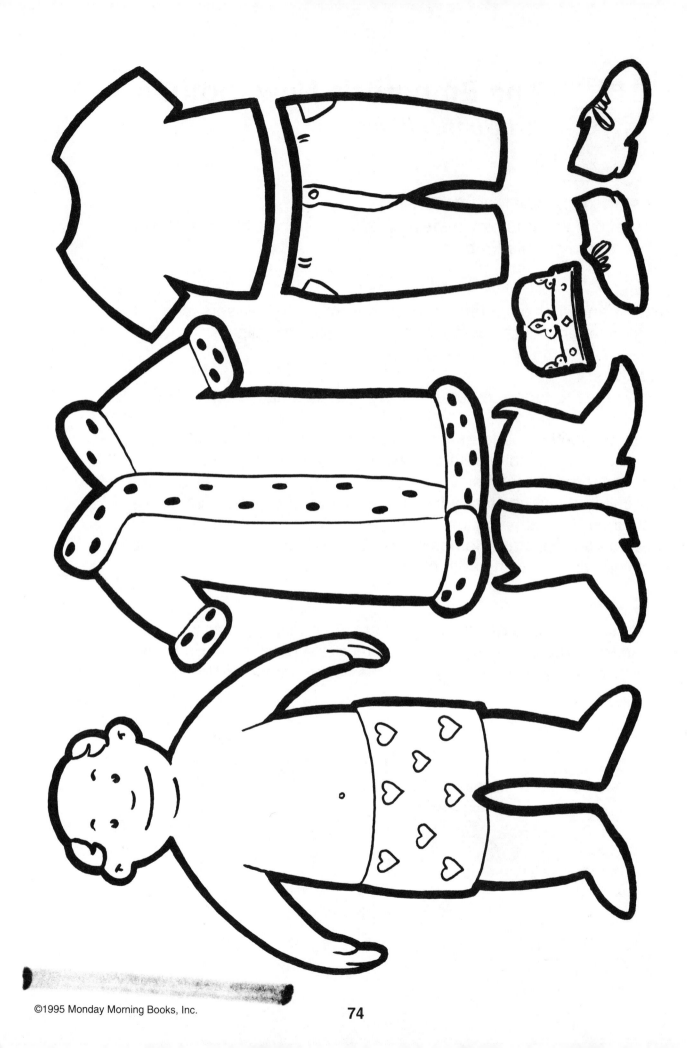

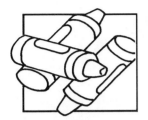

The Emperor's New Clothes
Art Connection

SEE-THROUGH EMPEROR

Materials:
Emperor pattern (p. 74), Emperor paper dolls (p. 73), overhead projector, transparencies, permanent marker, washable markers

Directions:
1. Trace the Emperor pattern onto a transparency using a permanent marker.
2. Have students place additional transparencies over their Emperor paper dolls and let them draw clothes using washable markers. (You can use several transparencies for the children, allowing for clean-off time between students.)
3. Place these child-designed clothes on top of the Emperor transparency, and put on an overhead projector fashion show for the class.

The Emperor's New Clothes
Math Connection

WEAR IT OUT!
Introduce this activity by reading *Mary Wore Her Red Dress and Henry Wore His Green Sneakers,* adapted and illustrated by Merle Peek (Clarion, 1985).

Materials:
Clothing patterns (p. 77), colored markers, large sheet of paper (for graph), tape

Directions:
1. Duplicate the clothing patterns so that every child has a copy.
2. Duplicate one extra set and make a six-column graph using clothing patterns.
3. Let children color in their patterns matching the clothing that they are wearing on the day that you do this activity. For example, a child wearing blue pants and a green top would color in those two patterns and tape them in the appropriate columns.
4. Have your students help you read the completed graph, and ask them questions, such as, "How many people have on blue shoes today?" Or, "How many people are wearing red shirts?"

MODEL BEHAVIOR
Students can take turns at being tailors and clothing models.

Materials:
Measuring tapes (soft ones), mirrors

Directions:
1. Have students measure each other from head to toe, including feet, hands, tummies, arms, etc.
2. Encourage children to have their model partners stand in front of a mirror while they make the different measurements, just like the charlatan tailors in the story. Children can then fit their models with dress-up clothes.

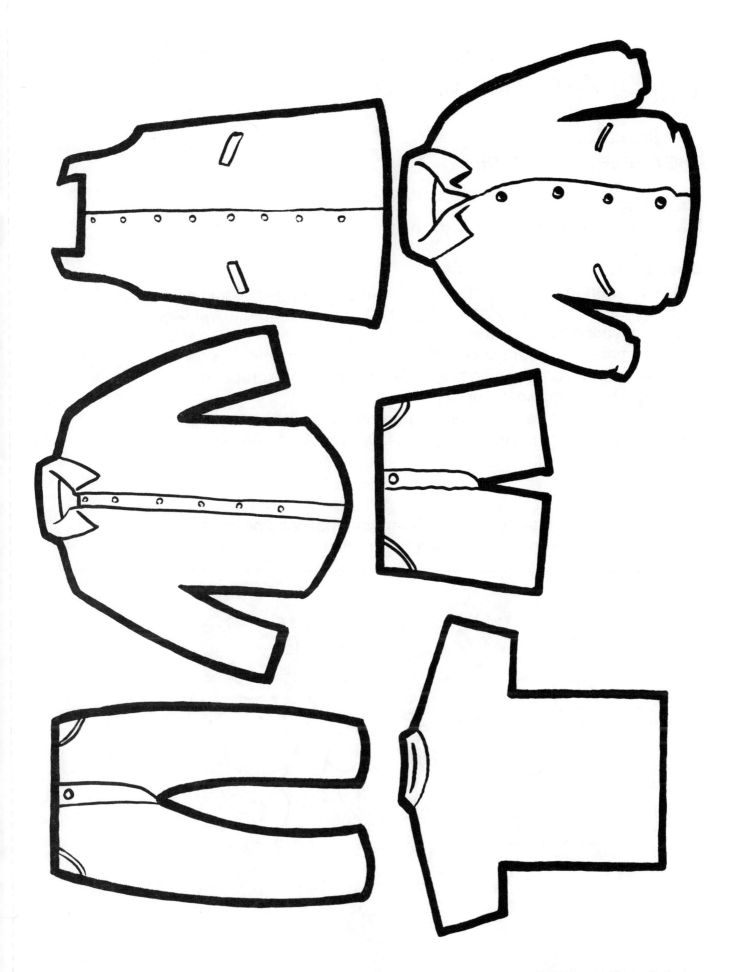

The Emperor's New Clothes
Games Connection

THE EMPEROR'S PARADE

Materials:
Marching music, paper crowns and hats

Directions:
1. Ask children to wear their most royal clothing on a specified day. You can suggest that they wear something red and purple (royal colors), or anything that they feel is special.
2. Hold a parade in your school yard, and have each child wear a crown or hat. Children should practice their royal walk: proper posture, head held high, knees up.
3. Parade for other classes, or invite parents to join in the fun. Play parade or marching music, such as *The Original All-American Sousa!* (Delos, 1990).

Option:
Let children help decorate with streamers and balloons before the parade. Make colored confetti with a hole punch.

The Emperor's New Clothes
Snack Connection

EMPEROR'S SALAD DRESSING
At least the Emperor's salad is dressed!

Ingredients:
Cut-up vegetables (carrot sticks, celery sticks, cucumber slices, cherry tomatoes, cauliflower and broccoli florets), assorted dressings (Ranch, Italian, French)

Directions:
1. You can tease your class by bringing in an empty plate and saying that only the smartest and most honorable students will be able to see this snack. (Expect a lot of laughter!)
2. Then bring out the "real" snack, cut-up vegetables and salad "dressing." Explain the pun to the children, and then let them choose which vegetables they want and which dressing they want to use for dipping. They can experiment with the different types to find the one they enjoy the most!

The Emperor's New Clothes
Resources

BOOKS

The Emperor's New Clothes by Hans Christian Andersen, retold by Anthea Bell, illustrated by Dorothee Dutze (North-South Books, 1986).
This is a formal, slightly oversized rendition of the famous tale.

The Emperor's New Clothes by Hans Christian Andersen, illustrated by Jack and Irene Delano (Random, 1971).
Have the children look for repeated patterns in groups on the pages.

The Emperor's New Clothes by Hans Christian Andersen, illustrated by Monika Laimgruber (Addison-Wesley, 1973).
This book features large, vividly colored illustrations done with a unique dot effect.

The Emperor's New Clothes by Hans Christian Andersen, adapted by Riki Levinson (Dutton, 1991).
Busy, detailed illustrations in an all-animal cast are special features in this version.

The Emperor's New Clothes by Hans Christian Andersen, illustrated by S.T. Mendelson (Stewart, Tabori and Chang, 1992).
The rich paintings done by Mendelson feature a gorilla as the Emperor.

The Emperor's New Clothes by Hans Christian Andersen, illustrated by Anne Rockwell (Harper, 1982).
This version is illustrated in Rockwell's classic style, with thin black pen lines and watercolor.

The Emperor's New Clothes by Hans Christian Andersen, adapted by Vera Southgate (Modern Curriculum Press, 1984). Originally, Macmillan, 1982.
This "Yellow Star" reader features this famous tale in an illustrated version for beginning readers.

The Emperor's New Clothes by Hans Christian Andersen, illustrated and adapted by Janet Stevens (Holiday, 1985).
In this version, the Emperor is a pig and the weavers are two sly foxes.

The Emperor's New Clothes by Hans Christian Andersen, illustrated by Nadine Bernard Wescott (Little, Brown, 1984).
This is a fun retelling of Andersen's famous story.

Mary Wore Her Red Dress and Henry Wore His Green Sneakers, adapted and illustrated by Merle Peek (Clarion, 1985).
The animal guests who attend Katy Bear's birthday party each wear different colored clothing. The story is very adaptable to the classroom. Add the names of your students and the color of clothes they are wearing.

The Principal's New Clothes by Stephanie Calmenson, illustrated by Denise Brunkus (Scholastic, 1989).
This is a funky modern version of *The Emperor's New Clothes*.

OTHER

The Emperor's New Clothes, read by Levar Burton (Durkin Hayes, 1994).
This cassette is part of the "Classic Tales" series.

The Emperor's New Clothes (SVS, 1990).
Read by Sir John Gielgud, music by Mark Isham, illustrated by Robert Van Nutt. This is a Rabbit Ears Production.

The Emperor's New Clothes (Warner, 1989).
A sly tailor teaches the Emperor a lesson.

The Emperor's New Clothes (Weston Woods, 1989).
In this classic videotape version, a vain emperor is swindled by two sly tailors.

Fisherman and His Wife

STORY SUMMARY

A kind fisherman catches a magic fish. In return for being set free, the fish offers to grant the man a wish. Unfortunately, the fisherman's greedy wife isn't satisfied with one measly wish. Her desires grow bigger and bigger, until her greed angers the fish. As a lesson, he returns the fisherwoman to her humble hovel—leaving her no better off than she was before she began her wishing spree.

SETTING THE STAGE: FANTASY FISHING!

Materials:

Fish patterns (p. 92), magnets, wooden poles or yardsticks, string, construction paper, scissors, aluminum foil, glue, glitter, paper clips, box or crate, foot stool

Directions:

- Let the children act out the parts of the story. They can take turns acting and being audience members.
- Simple props will enhance the play for your student actors. To make a fishing pole, attach a magnet to a long wooden pole or yardstick with a string. Cut colorful paper fish from the patterns and attach a paper clip to each one. Make one special "magic" fish and cover it with glitter or aluminum foil. The child who catches the magic fish can pretend to make a wish.
- Students can fish from a "boat" (an open box or crate), a "tree stump" (foot stool), and so on. Encourage them to use their imaginations.

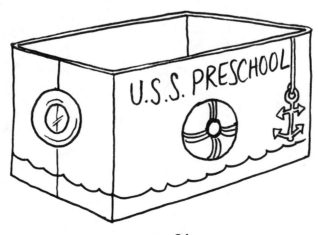

The Fisherman and His Wife
Learning Connection

F IS FOR FISHING . . .
Introduce the students to words that begin with "F," such as fish, fun, forest, fisherman, and foolish. Have the children brainstorm as many fabulous "F" words as they can.

FISHERMAN'S WRITING ASSIGNMENT
Duplicate the writing worksheet (p. 83) and give one to each child in the class. Have the children practice printing the letter "F" and words that begin with "F" by copying the examples given.

FISHERMAN'S FOLDER
Duplicate the folder cover (p. 84) and give one to each child. Children can use blue and green crayons to color the waves, and a variety of colored crayons, glue, and glitter for the fish. Have the children glue the pattern to the front of a manila folder. Children can keep all the work from this unit in their fisherman folder.

Foolish

fisherman

F

f

83

The Fisherman and His Wife
Art Connection

FISHY PRINTS

Materials:
Fresh real fish (see Discovery Connection, p. 88), tempera paint, paintbrush, white paper, scissors, stapler, paper towel roll cut into small sections (one section per child—each tube should provide for 5 children), tissue paper, hole punch, yarn

Directions:
1. Paint the fish with tempera paint and then press the white paper on top of it.
2. Make two prints per child, one from each side of the fish.
3. When the prints are dry, have the students cut them out.
4. Help the children staple the fish mouths around their section of paper towel roll (as shown), then staple closed the outer edges of the fish, leaving one small area open to allow for stuffing.
5. Show children how to stuff the fish with tissue paper and then staple closed the remaining opening.
6. Punch two holes in the mouth of each fish—through the paper towel tube ring—and thread with a length of yarn.

Option:
Hang the fishy prints from a clothesline strung across the classroom.

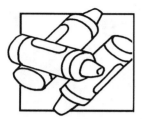

The Fisherman and His Wife
Art Connection

A FISH WISH

Materials:
Fish pattern (p. 87), crayons, white paper, glitter, glue

Directions:
1. Give each child a sheet of white paper.
2. Have the children close their eyes and imagine something that they really want.
3. Place a cut-out fish on each child's desk.
4. Tell the children to whisper their wish to the fish, and then to draw a picture of their wish on the paper. They can decorate their drawings with glitter and glue.
5. Post the completed "Fish Wish" pictures on a "Wishful Thinking" or "Wishful Fishing" bulletin board.
6. Write each child's name on the fish pattern and post the fish next to their pictures.

Option 1:
Have children write their wish on the fish pattern to post next to their drawings.

Option 2:
Read *The Rainbow Fish* by Marcus Pfister (North-South, 1992) to the students. Then provide aluminum foil or silvery paper for them to glue to the fish patterns for scales. The children can tell their wishes to these silvery fish.

The Fisherman and His Wife
Discovery Connection

SOMETHING'S FISHY!
This activity is best done outside. It's a good idea to have plenty of sudsy water and towels for use after this project.

Materials:
A fish (yes, a real one!)

Directions:
1. Purchase a fresh, whole fish at the market and bring it into the classroom.
2. Discuss the parts of the fish (tail, fins, gills), its texture, and its smell!
3. Allow children to gently touch, poke, and prod the fish.

Note: Save the fish for use during art time (see p. 85).

The Fisherman and His Wife
Discovery Connection

WHAT A WATER TABLE!

Materials:
Water table, plastic fish in a variety of sizes, small nets or strainers

Directions:
1. Float plastic fish in the water table.
2. Provide small strainers or nets for children to use to try and catch the plastic fish.
3. Let children describe the fish that they catch: "I caught one this big, but you should have seen the one that got away!"

Option:
Show children pictures of different types of fish from non-fiction books, such as *Do Fishes Get Thirsty?* Questions answered by the New England Aquarium (Franklin Watts, 1991). *Fish* by Steve Parker (Knopf, 1990) is part of the Eyewitness Book Series. It includes information about fish skeletons, swimming, tails and fins, feeding, and eggs.

The Fisherman and His Wife
Math Connection

I'VE GOT A WHOLE FISH IN MY HANDS

Materials:
Goldfish crackers, blue construction paper

Directions:
1. Divide a bag of Goldfish crackers among your class, giving each student ten to twenty crackers.
2. Give each child a sheet of blue construction paper to place on his or her desk. The blue can represent an ocean or lake, and the children can place the fish in their own ocean.
3. Tell simple story problems about the fish the children have in their ocean.
4. Let the children eat the crackers at the end of math time, or as you work through the problems.

One goldfish plus
one goldfish equals...

The Fisherman and His Wife
Games Connection

FISHING FOR FUN

Materials:
Construction paper, fish patterns (p. 92), scissors, magnets, string, yardsticks or wooden poles, plastic tub, marker, paper clips

Directions:
1. Cut out paper fish from a variety of colored construction paper.
2. Program the fish with vocabulary words.
3. Place a paper clip on each fish, and place fish in a plastic tub.
4. Make fishing poles by attaching magnets to long wooden poles or yardsticks with string.
5. Let children take turns fishing. When they catch a fish, have them read the word on the fish and use it in a sentence.
6. Let children keep the fish whose word they can correctly read, and throw the others back.
7. When a child has caught and correctly read all the "word fish," have him or her put all the fish back in the tub and let another child take a turn.

Option 1:
You can also program the fish with alphabet letters (in upper- and lower-case), numbers, or color words.

Option 2:
Play "Go Fish" with either a commercially produced game or a deck of cards. Good experience with sets of four.

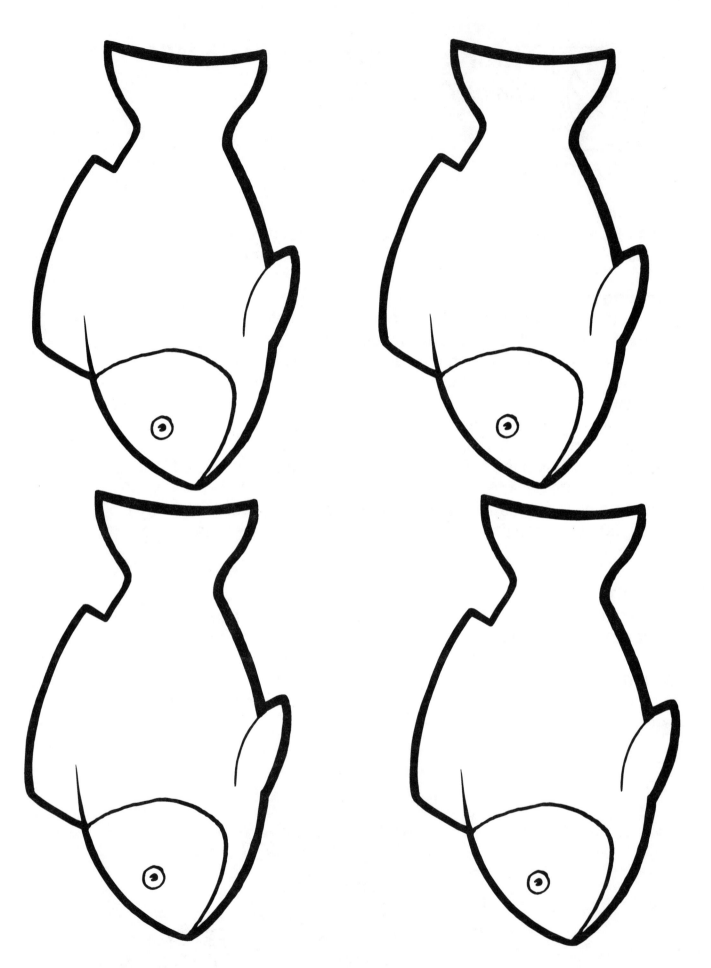

The Fisherman and His Wife
Snack Connection

APPLE SEA TURTLES

Ingredients:
Apples cut in half (one per child), peanut butter, raisins, banana slices, cut-up dried fruits and fresh fruits, paper plates, rounded plastic knives (for spreading peanut butter)

Directions:
1. Give each child an apple half.
2. Have the children set their apple half cut-side down on a paper plate.
3. Provide peanut butter, raisins, bananas, and other chopped fruits for children to use to decorate their turtle's "shell" and to add a head and legs.
4. When the children have finished decorating, they can eat their apple turtles.

Option:
Show pictures of sea turtles in a book such as *Fish* by Steve Parker (Knopf, 1990) in the Eyewitness Book Series.

The Fisherman and His Wife
Resources

BOOKS

Big Al by Andrew Clements, illustrated by Yoshi (Scholastic, 1988).
Wonderful illustrations by Yoshi and the brief text by Clements work together to tell the story of a big, ugly, and lonely fish who makes friends in the ocean.

Blue Sea by Robert Kalan, illustrated by Donald Crews (Greenwillow, 1979).
Big, bigger, biggest and small, smaller, and smallest are concepts introduced in this book.

Fish Is Fish by Leo Lionni (Pantheon, 1970).
When Fish dreams of a better life on land, his friend Frog comes to his aid. Short text on double-page illustrations.

The Fisherman and His Wife by the Grimm Brothers (Greenwillow, 1978).
Monika Laimgruber's large, colorful illustrations enhance this classic story.

The Fisherman and His Wife by the Grimm Brothers, retold by John Warren Stewig, illustrated by Margot Tomes (Holiday House, 1988).
Finely detailed illustrations accompany the retold tale of a fisherman's greedy wife who is never satisfied with the wishes granted her by an enchanted fish.

Fishy Riddles by Katy Hall and Lisa Eisenberg, illustrated by Simms Taback (Dial, 1983).
Silly illustrations and an easy-to-read text make this book perfect for the early-reader age group.

The Little Fish That Got Away by Bernadine Cook, illustrated by Crockett Johnson (Scholastic, 1956).
A little boy finally succeeds at fishing in this charming tale.

The Magic Fish by Freya Littledale (Scholastic, 1985).
A fisherman catches a wish-granting fish, but his wife is never satisfied.

The Magic Fish Rap by Bernice and Jon Chardiet (Scholastic, 1993).
The tale of the fisherman and his greedy wife is retold in rollicking, rhyming rap verses with a cassette featuring rap on one side and reading on the other.

Nessa's Fish by Nancy Luenn (Atheneum, 1990).
Magical pictures illustrate Nessa's ingenuity and bravery. She foils animal poachers to save the fish she and her grandmother caught to feed everyone in their Eskimo camp.

The Ocean Alphabet Book by Jerry Pallotta (Charlesbridge, 1986).
Brightly colored illustrations and accurate scientific information make this a very special A to Z. Also by this author: *The Underwater Alphabet* (Trumpet Club, 1991), with spectacular illustrations by Edgar Stewart.

Ocean Parade: A Counting Book by Patricia MacCarthy (Dial, 1990).
An array of brightly colored fish introduce numbers from one through one hundred and the concepts of size and shape.

A Patchwork Fish Tale by Stewart Mokowitz (Simon and Schuster, 1982).
This is a story of how a greedy fish in the aquarium acquires interesting patches.

That's Not Goldie by Miriam Schlein (Simon and Schuster, 1990).
A goldfish named Goldie, believed to be dead, is flushed down the toilet. She escapes through the sewer system and into the goldfish pond at the botanical garden.

# **G**ingerbread Man

STORY SUMMARY
A little old woman bakes a gingerbread cookie for her husband. Before he can be eaten, the gingerbread man jumps off the cookie tin and runs away. He taunts all the creatures he passes, shouting to each, "I'll run and run as fast as I can! You can't catch me, I'm the gingerbread man!" However, his luck runs out when a sly fox tricks him and gobbles him up!

SETTING THE STAGE: GLORIOUS GINGERBREAD!

Materials:
Wigs, old knee socks, cotton stuffing, safety pin, paper plates, hole punch, yarn, brown paint, paintbrush, rubber animal noses, animal costumes

Directions:
- Have student groups reenact this fun tale. Bring in a couple of wigs for the little old woman and the little old man. Make a simple fox tail by stuffing a red or brown knee sock with cotton and tying it closed. It can be attached with a safety pin to a child's waistband. Visit a costume or display store for durable animal noses. Children may also be able to lend old Halloween costumes for the play.
- Make gingerbread boy masks from paper plates (see p. 99).
- If possible, videotape the skits and play them back while the class devours their cookies (see p. 105). You can also play these skits for parents during open house.

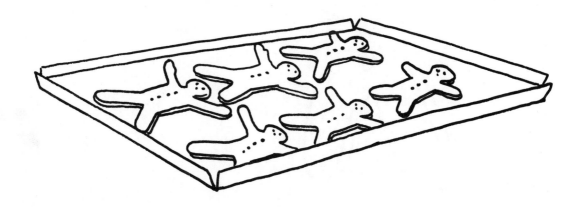

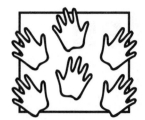

Gingerbread Man
Learning Connection

G IS FOR . . .

Introduce the students to words that begin with "G," such as gingerbread, go, grandma, and grandpa. Emphasize all of the words that begin with the hard "G" sound ("grapes") and the soft "G" sound ("ginger"). Have the children brainstorm as many great "G" words as they can.

GINGERBREAD MAN'S WRITING ASSIGNMENT

Duplicate the writing worksheet (p. 97) and give one to each child in the class. Have the children practice printing the letter "G" and words that begin with "G" by copying the examples given.

GINGERBREAD MAN'S FOLDER

Duplicate the folder cover (p. 98) and give one to each child to color and glue to the front of a manila folder. Provide sequins, glitter, and glue for children to use to decorate their folders. Children can keep all the work from this unit in their folder.

Gingerbread
Good
Grandmother
go
great

Gingerbread

good

G

g

98

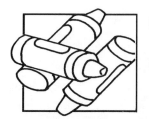

Gingerbread Man
Art Connection

GINGERBREAD MAN MASKS

Materials:
Paper plates (one per child), brown paint, paintbrushes, crayons, markers, colored chalk, construction paper, glue, scissors, Popsicle sticks or hole punch and yarn

Directions:
1. Give each child a paper plate that has two large holes cut out for the eyes. (Older children will be able to do this themselves.)
2. Provide brown paint and brushes to the children to use to paint their mask a warm gingerbread shade.
3. Once the plates have dried, set out markers, chalk, and crayons for children to use to decorate their gingerbread masks. They can also cut shapes from colored construction paper to glue on for decorations.
4. Children can glue a Popsicle stick to their mask for a handle, or punch a hole on either side of the mask and thread through with a length of yarn for a tie.

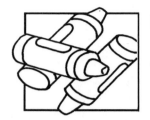

Gingerbread Man
Art Connection

GINGERBREAD MAN PUPPETS

Materials:
Gingerbread man and character patterns (p. 101), tagboard or oak tag, yarn, buttons, wiggly eyes, glue, Popsicle sticks, scissors

Directions:
1. Copy the gingerbread patterns onto tagboard or oak tag and cut out.
2. Let children decorate the characters with yarn and buttons.
3. Provide wiggly eyes for children to glue to their patterns.
4. Show children how to glue Popsicle sticks to the back of their patterns to make hand puppets.
5. Children can put on a puppet show using their gingerbread man-theme stick puppets.

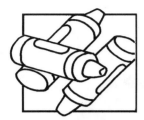

Gingerbread Man
Art Connection

PLAYING WITH PLAYDOUGH

Materials:
Playdough in a variety of colors, gingerbread man and related cookie cutters, rolling pins and other kitchen utensils

Directions:
1. Let children experiment with rolling pins and various kitchen utensils to roll out a variety of colored playdough.
2. Provide assorted cookie cutters for children to use to cut out gingerbread men and other characters from the story.

Option 1:
Use baker's dough, and let it dry after children mold it into desired shapes. Provide paints and brushes for children to use to paint their creations.

Option 2:
Let children work with real gingerbread, and decorate it with cake decorations, red hots, raisins, etc.

Gingerbread Man
Math Connection

GINGERBREAD MATH

Materials:
Gingerbread man cookie cutter, card stock, scissors

Directions:
1. Trace a gingerbread cutter onto heavy card stock and cut out multiple manipulatives.
2. Give each child several of the manipulatives.
3. Lead the children through math problems that they can work out using the gingerbread men manipulatives.

Option 1:
Discuss the numbers in a gingerbread cookie recipe and let the students measure out the ingredients into a pan or bowl.

Option 2:
Buy a box of miniature gingerbread men for an edible math lesson.

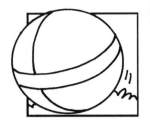

Gingerbread Man
Games Connection

GINGERBREAD RACING

Directions:
1. Designate certain children to play different characters from the story: the little old woman, little old man, variety of animals including the fox.
2. Position the characters in different spots on the playground, for example, at the bottom of the slide, near the monkey bars, by the swings, and so on.
3. Have the rest of the children run through an obstacle course, past the old woman, man, and animals. Direct them to use each piece of playground equipment that is near the characters.
4. Let the children take turns playing the different roles.

Note: Have the children acting out the characters remind the other children of what they should do in the obstacle course. For example, if the "little old woman" is standing by the slide, she should say, "Slide down the slide before going on to the next station."

Option:
Play Gingerbread Tag. Have all the children start as gingerbread men except one. That child should be the fox and should chase the gingerbread men. As the gingerbread men are caught, they become additional foxes. The last gingerbread man caught becomes the first fox in the next round.

Gingerbread Man
Snack Connection

GINGERBREAD COOKIES

Ingredients:
Pre-made gingerbread cookie dough, raisins, currants, cinnamon candies, white icing, rolling pins, gingerbread-theme cookie cutters

Directions:
1. With extra help from parents or older students, roll and cut out the cookie dough.
2. Let the students decorate their own character with raisins, currants, cinnamon candies, and white icing.

Option:
1. Make up a package of gingerbread in cake form.
2. Have the children compare the gingerbread cake with the cookies. Ask them what they think makes the two the same and different. Ask which kind of gingerbread your students would want to have again.
3. Make a two-column graph of the children's preferences, letting them use a rubber stamp or stickers to mark their gingerbread choice.

Note: Be sure to include a discussion of kitchen safety, ingredients, and measuring techniques.

Gingerbread Man
Resources

BOOKS

The Baby's Story Book by Kay Chorao (E. P. Dutton, 1985).
This great resource includes fifteen familiar folk tales and fables with animals as the characters, short text, and sweet illustrations.

The Gingerbread Boy by William Curtis Holdsworth (Farrar, 1968).
The traditional tale is told in pages of partial text with black and white illustrations.

The Gingerbread Boy by Paul Galdone (Clarion Books, 1975).
The traditional tale of the bragging gingerbread boy is told in the fun Galdone fashion.

The Gingerbread Man by Fran Hunia, illustrated by Brian Price Thomas (Ladybird, 1977).
This is in the read-it-yourself series.

The Gingerbread Man by Eric A. Kimmel, illustrated by Megan Lloyd (Holiday, 1993).
A freshly baked cookie outwits many animals until he meets a clever fox.

Johnny-Cake by Joseph Jacobs (Putnam's, 1933).
A rolling pancake can outrun everyone except the wolf! This is a very similar story to the tale of the Gingerbread Man.

The Stinky Cheese Man and Other Fairly Stupid Tales by Jon Scieszka, illustrated by Lane Smith (Viking, 1992).
These fractured fairy tales, such as "The Really Ugly Duckling," are inventive retellings of traditional stories.

You Can't Catch Me! by Joanne Oppenheim (Houghton Mifflin, 1986).
This book is a good extension for either *The Gingerbread Man* or *The Old Lady and the Fly*, as a pesky black fly taunts all the animals. He boasts that the other creatures cannot catch him, but he bothers one too many. Fun tale told in rhyme with unusual illustrations and cumulative text.

Humpty Dumpty

STORY SUMMARY

Humpty Dumpty sat on a wall.
Humpty Dumpty had a great fall.
All the King's horses,
And all the King's men,
Couldn't put Humpty
Together again!

SETTING THE STAGE: HUMPTY'S HOME

Materials:

Play phone, old sheet or white cloth, scissors

Directions:

- This is a good lead-in for a discussion about what to do during an emergency. Provide a play phone for students to use to practice dialing the rescue number for your area.
- Invite a member of an emergency rescue service into your classroom to discuss emergency procedures.
- Put on a mini-Humpty Dumpty performance piece. Designate one child as Humpty Dumpty. Half of the rest of the children can act as the King's horses and the others as the King's men. Provide strips of an old sheet or white cloth for children to use for bandaging Humpty.

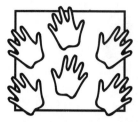

Humpty Dumpty
Learning Connection

H IS FOR HUMPTY . . .
Introduce the students to words that begin with "H," such as horses, Humpty, hard-boiled, hurry, hectic, and hurt. Have the children brainstorm as many "H" words as they can.

HUMPTY'S WRITING ASSIGNMENT
Duplicate the writing worksheet (p. 109) and give one to each child in the class. Have the children practice printing the letter "H" and words that begin with "H" by copying the examples given or choosing from the brainstormed list.

HUMPTY'S FOLDER
Duplicate the brick wall folder cover (p. 110) for the students to color, decorate, and glue to the front of a manila folder. Have the children tape Humpty to the top of their activity folder. Children can keep all the work for this unit in their folder.

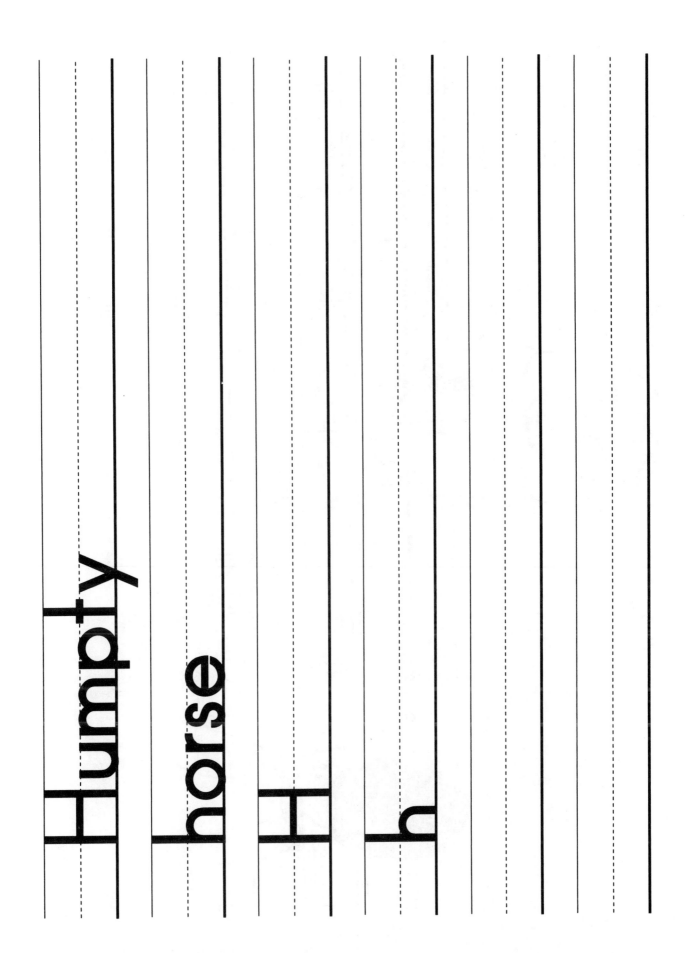

Humpty

horse

H

h

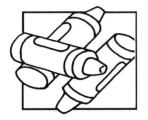

Humpty Dumpty
Art Connection

HUMPTY'S CRACKED UP!

Materials:
Puzzle (p. 112), heavy paper, crayons, glue, card stock, scissors, spray adhesive (optional)

Directions:
1. Duplicate the puzzle page onto heavy paper for each student.
2. Have the students color Humpty and glue him onto card stock. (If possible, let an aide or parent helper use a spray adhesive for a quick and firm hold.)
3. After Humpty dries, have the students cut along the dotted lines to form puzzle pieces. The middle is a special surprise—the letter "H."
4. Challenge the students to put Humpty together again.

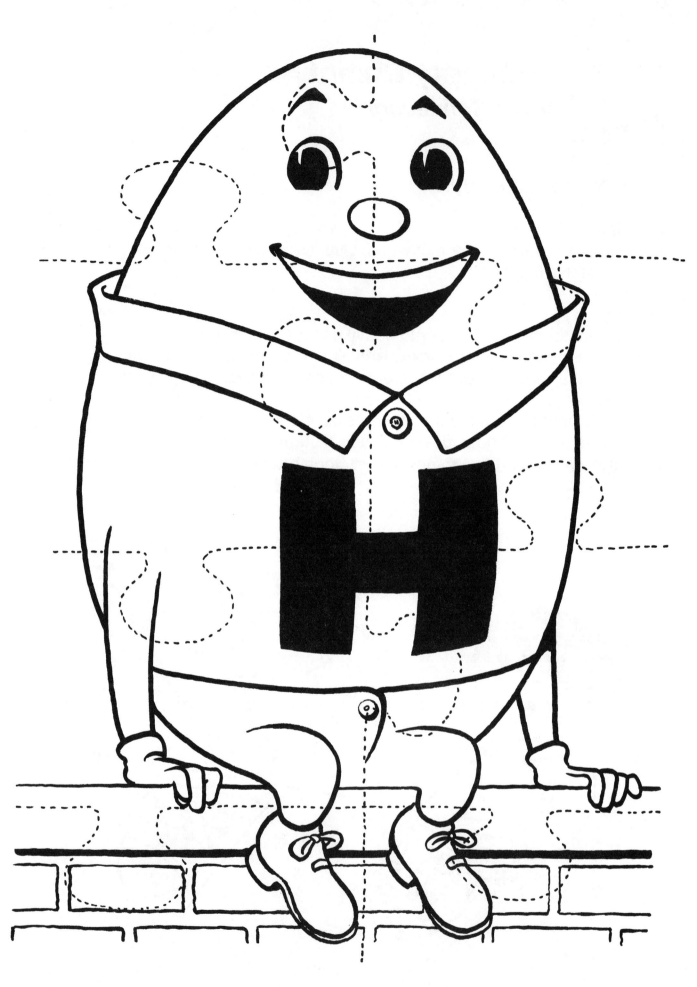

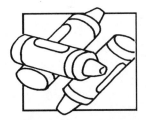

Humpty Dumpty
Art Connection

HOORAY FOR HUMPTY!

Materials:
Easel paper, easels, clothespins or clips, tempera paint in assorted colors, paintbrushes, glitter, glue, construction paper, scissors

Directions:
1. Cut egg shapes from large easel paper.
2. Clip the egg shapes to easels.
3. Provide an assortment of colored tempera paints for children to use to paint their eggs.
4. Once the egg paintings have dried, let the students glue on decorations. They can cut out shapes from construction paper to glue to the eggs. Or they can dot their paintings with glue and sprinkle on multicolored glitter.
5. Post the completed egg paintings on a "Hooray for Humpty!" bulletin board.

Option:
Staple or tape a rubber band to the top of each egg painting and use thumbtacks to attach the paintings to the bulletin board. Children can gently pull on the bottom of the paintings to make the egg shapes bounce.

Humpty Dumpty
Discovery Connection

RUBBERY EGGS

This experiment is fascinating, egg-citing, and easy!

Materials:

One hard-cooked egg, one raw egg, two clear plastic cups, vinegar, spoon

Directions:

1. Place each egg in its own plastic cup.
2. Cover both eggs with vinegar.
3. Stir gently every so often during the next three days. The calcium will dissolve from the outer shell of the eggs.
4. Ask the children the following questions:
   • Do the cooked egg and the uncooked egg look the same?
   • What happens when you touch the "rubbery" eggs?

Option:

Check out pages 36-38 in the book *Why Can't You Unscramble An Egg?* by Vicki Cobb, illustrated by Ted Enik (Dutton, 1990) for an explanation (in "kid terms") of chemical reactions.

Humpty Dumpty
Discovery Connection

THE YOKE'S ON US!

Materials:
Six eggs, plastic tarp, paper, non-toxic markers

Directions:
1. Hard boil three of the eggs, and leave the other three eggs uncooked.
2. Number the eggs from 1 to 6 with a non-toxic marker.
3. Discuss the word "fragile" with the students.
4. Spread a plastic tarp on the floor, and let the students carefully examine the eggs while standing on the tarp.
5. Have students guess which eggs are cooked and which eggs are raw.
6. Help them write their predictions on pieces of paper.
7. Drop the numbered eggs off the edge of a "wall" (table top) onto the tarp below.
8. Let students check their prediction sheets. Ask them how many eggs they guessed correctly.

Humpty Dumpty
Math Connection

EGG CARTON MATH

Materials:
Egg carton, permanent marker, plastic eggs, buttons (or other small manipulatives)

Directions:
1. Write numerals from 1 to 12 on the inside bottom of the sections of the egg carton.
2. Number plastic eggs (available at Easter time) from 1 to 12.
3. Set out buttons or other small manipulatives.
4. Have the students fill each plastic egg with the correct number of buttons (or other materials), and then place the eggs in the correct spaces in the carton.
5. Check each student's work before having the child empty the eggs for the next student's use.

Humpty Dumpty
Math Connection

EGG-CITING CHART

Materials:
Egg patterns (p. 118), scissors, markers, tape, white paper, crayons

Directions:
1. Duplicate the patterns and cut out.
2. Make a graph on a large sheet of white paper and post the graph on a bulletin board.
3. Have the children choose the pattern that is closest to how they like their eggs.
4. Let the children color in their pattern with crayons before posting the pattern in the correct column.
5. Help the students read their "Egg-Citing Chart."

Option:
Have the children survey friends in other classes or family members regarding their preferences for eating eggs. Add this information to the chart.

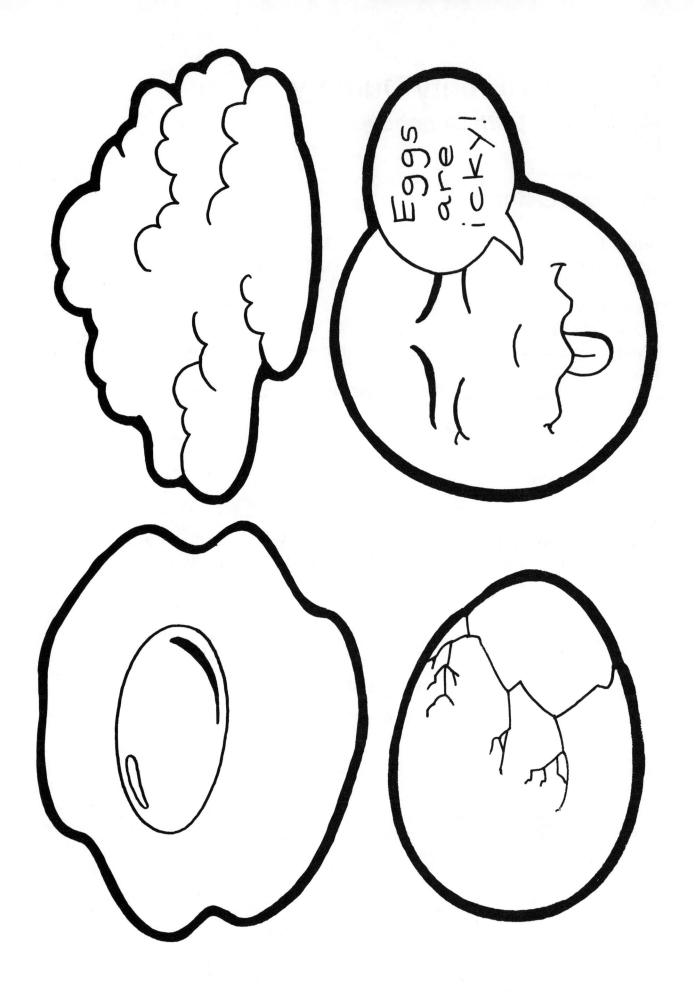

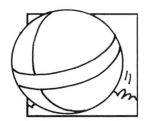

Humpty Dumpty
Games Connection

HUMPTY DUMPTY SAT ON A WALL!

Directions:
1. Have the children sit cross-legged on the floor and close their eyes.
2. Tell them to imagine that they are all Humpty Dumpties sitting on the edge of a wall and that they must balance so that they don't fall.
3. Then have them rock back and forth as if they are losing their balance.
4. Finally, have them roll all the way over (to one side or the other), as if they have lost their balance completely and rolled off the wall.
5. The children can yell, "Splat!" when they fall over.

Option:
Have the class chant the Mother Goose rhyme while they are rocking.

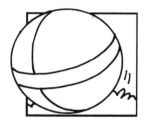

Humpty Dumpty
Games Connection

EGG RACE

Materials:
Plastic eggs, masking tape

Directions:
1. Use masking tape to make start and finish lines on the floor.
2. Have children push a plastic egg across the floor with their noses.

Note: This can be done as a relay race, but do it for fun—no winners or losers!

Option:
Hide the plastic eggs around the room or in the playground and let children team up in pairs to find them.

Humpty Dumpty
Snack Connection

GREEN EGGS AND HAM

Materials:
Eggs, green food coloring, *Green Eggs and Ham* by Dr. Seuss

Directions:
1. Cook eggs in a variety of ways: scrambled, poached, hard boiled, and green!
2. Let the children sample the different varieties.
3. As they eat their snack, read *Green Eggs and Ham* by Dr. Seuss, or show the very entertaining video based on the book.

Option:
Tell the children this Mother Goose riddle while they eat their snack:

AN EGG
> In marble halls as white as milk,
> Lined with a skin as soft as silk,
> Within a fountain crystal-clear,
> A golden apple doth appear.
> No doors there are to this stronghold,
> Yet thieves break in and steal the gold.

Humpty Dumpty
Resources

BOOKS

Chicken Tricks by Megan Lloyd (Harper and Row, 1983).
Once a month, playful hens substitute fake, but very innovative, eggs for the ones they are expected to lay. The farmer puts up with their shenanigans until December, when the joke is on them!

Cluck One by Louise Mathews (Dodd, Mead, 1982).
Cute illustrations show a weasel sneaking an assortment of animal eggs into Mrs. Cluck's nest, while the unknowing hen eagerly awaits their hatching.

An Egg Is for Wishing by Helen Kay (Abelard-Schuman, 1966).
This is the story of Nicholas, who overcomes his fear of chickens and then goes through the process of elaborately decorating Easter eggs.

The Great Big Especially Beautiful Easter Egg by James Stevenson (Scholastic, 1983).
Stevenson, in typical form, blends Grandpa's tall tales in a combination of text and cartoon-captioned illustrations for a special Easter whopper for the grandchildren.

Green Eggs and Ham by Dr. Seuss (Random House, 1960).
This children's classic is a good book for beginning readers.

Humpty Dumpty by Rodney Peppe (Viking Kestrel, 1974).
Though all the king's men can't get Humpty together again after the fall, the reader is given the opportunity to do so. This story is told in large type, brief text, and colorful illustrations.

It Wasn't My Fault by Helen Lester (Houghton Mifflin, 1985).

This is a humorously illustrated account of Murdley Gurdson's experience with a bird who lays an egg on his head. Although accidents are usually Murdley's own fault, in this situation he tries hard to blame someone else.

The Mare's Egg by Carole Spray (Camden House, 1981).
A man, fooled by his neighbor, is pleased with how events turn out for him in the long run, and is prepared to be duped again.

The Most Wonderful Egg in the World by Helme Heine (Macmillan, 1983).
When the king must settle a quarrel between hens, he chooses the one who lays the most beautiful egg. Told through wonderfully non-sensical illustrations and short text.

The Pinkish, Purplish, Bluish Egg by Bill Peet (Houghton Mifflin, 1963).
With a rhyming text of half a page per double-page illustration, a tale is told of a griffin hatching from a special egg.

Rechenka's Eggs by Patricia Polacco (Philomel Books, 1988).
Polacco's magic touch is evident in this story about an injured goose rescued by Babushka. The goose, having broken the eggs in the Easter Festival, lays thirteen marvelously colored eggs to replace them. She leaves behind one final miracle in egg form before returning to her own land.

Sing Me a Story by Jane Browne (Crown, 1991).
This book features thirteen songs based on well-known nursery rhymes and fairy tales. Instructions for making action movements accompany each song.

Itsy Bitsy Spider

STORY SUMMARY

The itsy, bitsy spider climbed up the waterspout.
Down came the rain and washed the spider out.
Out came the sun and dried up all the rain,
And the itsy bitsy spider climbed up the spout again.

SETTING THE STAGE: INCREDIBLE SPIDERS

Materials:

Construction paper, large sheet of white paper, marker, string, yarn, small tokens, fiberfill, paper punch, *Charlotte's Web*, plastic spider rings, plastic waterspout, cardboard, scissors, chalkboard, chalk

Directions:

- This is a great opportunity to learn about arachnids. Ask your students to dictate everything that they know about spiders. Write their ideas on a web shape drawn on a large sheet of paper. Add to the chart as the students progress through the unit.
- With string, yarn, or fiberfill, students can spin their own webs. Provide a plastic waterspout, a cardboard sun, and some confetti raindrops (students can make their own with a paper punch), and students are ready to reenact this favorite rhyme.
- Spider rings are usually available inexpensively in October, and are a very fun prop. Buy them on sale in early November and save for your unit.
- Wrap yarn around small items that are in a story you read and unwrap the yarn ball as the story is told, allowing the items to fall out in the correct sequence.
- Older students will love the story of *Charlotte's Web*. Read a chapter a day to them. Draw a simple "Charlotte's web" on a chalkboard in the room. Write special messages to your students via the web, as Charlotte did for Wilbur.

Incredible

123

Itsy Bitsy Spider
Learning Connection

I IS FOR ITSY . . .

Introduce the students to words that begin with "I," such as itsy, ill, investigate, inside, and islands. Have the children brainstorm as many "I" words as they can.

A IS FOR . . .

"Arachnophobia" is an excellent vocabulary word. As a class, brainstorm reasons why people might be afraid of spiders. Tell the children that not all spiders are dangerous to humans. Challenge the children to think about the ways that spiders help us.

ITSY'S WRITING ASSIGNMENT

Duplicate the writing worksheet (p. 125) and give one to each child in the class. Have the children practice printing the letter "I" and words that begin with "I" by copying the examples given.

ITSY'S FOLDER

Duplicate the folder cover (p. 126) and give one to each child to color and glue to the front of a manila folder. Provide silver watercolors or aluminum foil for children to use to make the waterspout.
Children can keep all the work from this unit in their folder.

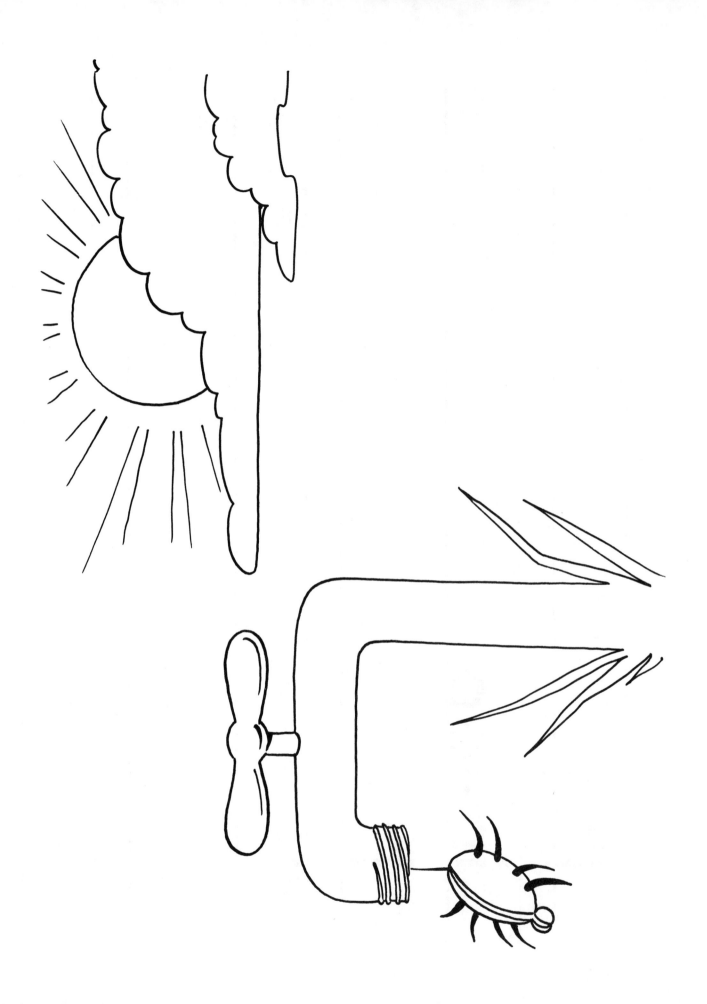

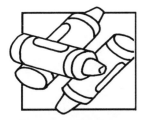

Itsy Bitsy Spider
Art Connection

ITSY BITSY T-SHIRT

Materials:
T-shirts (one per child), fabric paints in squeeze bottles, plastic spiders (one per child), glue gun

Directions:
1. Ask each student to bring a dark-colored T-shirt from home.
2. Provide fabric paints in squeeze bottles for children to use to draw webs on the shirts.
3. Glue a plastic spider to the shirt with a hot-melt glue gun.

Note: An art room helper is essential for this activity.

Option:
Let children wear their T-shirts in an "Incredible Itsy Bitsy Spider Parade!"

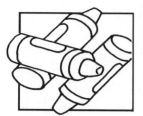

Itsy Bitsy Spider
Art Connection

SPIDER PAINTING

Materials:
Black construction paper, marbles (one per child), paints (silver and white), pie tins (or box lids), black crayons, newspapers, silver glitter (optional), spider stickers (optional)

Directions:
1. Tell children that they will be "marble painting."
2. Set out black paper and tins of white or silver paint on tables covered with newspaper. (Add a little bit of glitter to the paint for shimmering webs.)
3. Show the children how to dip their marbles in the tins of paint and then roll their marbles across their papers to make thin, spider web-like lines.
4. Have the students rotate their papers as they continue to "marble paint," covering the whole sheet with the webby designs.
5. After students' webs dry, they can put a spider sticker onto them. Or have children draw a spider on their web with black crayons.
6. Post the completed paintings on a "Charlotte's Cousins" bulletin board.

SPIDER MAKING

Materials:
Black balloons, paper, tape

Directions:
1. Blow up black balloons.
2. Fold strips of paper in accordion folds and tape eight legs onto each balloon.

Itsy Bitsy Spider
Math Connection

INSECT ARITHMETIC

Materials:
Buggy patterns (p. 130), large sheet of paper, glue, crayons, scissors

Directions:
1. Duplicate the buggy patterns and make a chart with an insect at the top of each column.
2. Let the children choose which insect is their favorite. They can color and cut out the pattern of the insect they like best.
3. Have the children glue their pattern into the correct column in the chart.
4. Help the children read the insect charts.

Option:
Let children use the buggy patterns to glue to a web. Have them glue a spider pattern in the center. Use the patterns to make up math problems, for example, "If the spider caught three moths and two flies, how many bugs did it catch?" Older children can create their own math problems.

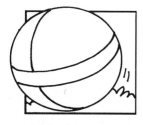

Itsy Bitsy Spider
Games Connection

SPIDER WALK

Directions:
1. Divide students into teams of four.
2. Have the children form a train by placing their hands on the waist of the person in front of them.
3. Encourage the children to try walking together like a spider.

SPIDER WEB

Materials:
Embroidery floss or yarn

Directions:
1. Use a different color of embroidery floss or yarn for each student, and tie a prize, such as a spider ring, at one end of each thread.
2. Weave the threads around the room, creating a colorful web.
3. Have each student follow a thread, winding it into a ball as he or she works to the end to gain a prize.

Option:
Show children pictures of actual spiders and spider webs before embarking on this game. Four-color photographic books on spiders include *Eight Legs* by D. M. Souza (Carolrhoda, 1991) and *Spiders* by Timothy Levi Biel (Creative Education, 1985).

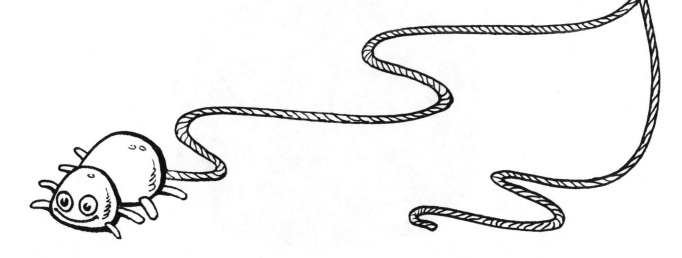

Itsy Bitsy Spider
Snack Connection

SPIDER SNACK

Ingredients:
Black licorice wheels or large black gumdrops, black licorice whip

Directions:
1. Have the children use the black licorice wheels or large black gumdrops for a spider's body sections.
2. Set out short sections of black licorice whip for the children to use for legs.

SPIDER WEBS

Ingredients:
Cake or cookies, frosting (chocolate or another dark-colored frosting), white icing or marshmallow creme, knife

Directions:
1. Frost a cake or cookies with a dark-colored frosting.
2. Use white icing or marshmallow creme to pipe concentric circles on the cake or cookies.
3. Take a knife and run it through the top surface of the piping starting in the middle, moving outward in six or eight lines around the cake or cookies.

Itsy Bitsy Spider
Resources

BOOKS

The Adventures of Spider: West African Folktales by Joyce Cooper Arkhurst, illustrated by Jerry Pinkney (Little, Brown, 1964). This book explains how Spider got a thin waist and a bald head, as well as why he lives in ceilings and dark corners.

Anansi and the Moss-Covered Rock by Eric Kimmel, illustrated by Janet Stevens (Holiday House, 1988).
Anansi the spider uses a strange moss-covered rock in the forest to trick all of the other animals, until little Bush Deer decides to teach Anansi a lesson.

Anansi Goes Fishing by Eric Kimmel, illustrated by Janet Stevens (Holiday House, 1992). Anansi the spider plans to trick Turtle into catching a fish for his dinner, but Turtle is the one who ends up with a free meal. This story explains the origin of spider webs.

Anansi the Spider: A Tale from Ashanti by Gerald McDermott (Holt, 1972).
Colorful graphics and short text explain how the moon came to be in the sky.

Anansi: The Spider Man by Philip M. Sherlack, illustrated by Marcia Brown (Crowell, 1954).
Good teacher information, but too long for reading to young students.

Charlotte's Web by E. B. White (Harper and Row, 1952).
Charlotte, a web-writing spider, saves the life of her dear friend, Wilbur the pig. This 184-page chapter book has delighted readers for generations.

A Golden Guide: Spiders and Their Kin by Herbert Levi (Golden Press, 1990).
160 pages of detailed information and color illustrations of spiders.

How Spider Saved Christmas by Robert Krauss (Windmill, 1970).
Spider's Christmas presents to Ladybug and Fly are used to prevent a disaster.

Incy Wincy Spider by Colin and Jacqui Hawkins (Viking, 1985).
Children will love the pop-up surprise on the last page of this book. Instructions for a finger game to accompany the rhyme are included.

Itsy Bitsy Spider by Ida Trapani (Whispering Coyote Press, 1993).
The spider encounters a mouse, a cat, a rocking chair, and other obstacles as she makes her way to the top of a tree to spin her web.

The Lady and the Spider by Faith McNulty (Harper and Row, 1986).
A spider who lives in a head of lettuce is saved when the lady who finds her returns her to the garden. This is a cute book for an intended audience aged 4 to 8.

Someone Saw a Spider: Spider Facts and Folktales by Shirley Climo (Crowell, 1985).
This collection of myths, folklore, and superstitions about spiders from around the world includes interesting teacher information.

Spiders by Dorothy Childs Hogner (Crowell, 1955).
This book boasts 56 pages of text and black and white illustrations all about spiders.

Itsy Bitsy Spider
Resources

Spider Magic by Dorothy Hinshaw Patent (Holiday House, 1982).
In this book, the characteristics, behavior, and special organs of different spiders are described. Included is information about the water spider, orb spider, black widow, and tarantula.

A Spider Might by Tom Walther (Sierra Club Books, 1978).
Here is a description of the habitats and characteristics of spiders and the natural histories of twenty species commonly found in urban and suburban locations.

Spider Silk by Augusta Golden (Crowell, 1964).
A "Let's Read and Find Out Book" with simple text and illustrations.

Spider Watching by David Webster (Julian Messner, 1984).
This book offers a close look at spiders and spider webs, explaining how spiders live and reproduce and how they serve a useful purpose by eating insect pests.

Three Brave Women by C. L. G. Martin (Macmillan, 1991).
Mama and Grammy's humorous childhood anecdotes help Caitlin come to terms with her fear of spiders.

The Very Busy Spider by Eric Carle (Philomel Books, 1984).
The farm animals try to divert a busy little spider from spinning her web, but she persists and produces a thing of both beauty and usefulness. This popular book is available in several sizes.

OTHER

Anansi the Spider: A Tale from the Ashanti, a Gerald McDermott film (Films Inc., 1989).
This animated film relates the adventures of Anansi, the trickster-hero of the Ashanti people of Ghana in West Africa.

Charlotte's Web (Paramount, 1988).
This animated version of E. B. White's story features the voices of Debbie Reynolds, Paul Lynde, Henry Gibson, and Agnes Moorehead.

The Heroic Climb of the Itsy Bitsy Spider by David Novak (A Telling Experience, 1991).
This sound recording includes six stories for the entire family.

Itsy, Bitsy Spider (Frank Schaffer poster #2322).
This poster is available at many school supply stores.

Mother Goose Stories (Lorimar Home Video, 1988).
This is part of the Jim Henson play-along video series, and includes "Little Miss Muffet," "Song of Sixpence," and "Little Boy Blue," all acted out by the muppets.

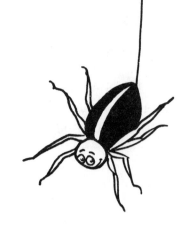

 # Jack and the Beanstalk

STORY SUMMARY

When poor Jack and his mother run out of money, Jack takes the family cow to the village to sell. Along the way, a trickster convinces Jack to trade his cow for three "magic" beans. Jack's mother, understandably upset with the trade, throws the beans out of the window where they take root and grow into a magic beanstalk. In the morning, Jack sees the beanstalk, and climbs it into the sky, where he meets a giant. Brave Jack steals the giant's gold, a goose that lays golden eggs, and a singing harp. Jack quickly climbs back down the beanstalk and chops it down before the giant can follow.

SETTING THE STAGE: GROWING A BEANSTALK

Materials:
Plastic cups, paper towels, beans, fabric bag, plastic eggs, poker chips, gold spray paint, paper, marker, book on growing beans

Directions:
- Give each child a clear plastic cup, a damp paper towel, and three beans. Have students place their beans in the cup with the crumpled, damp towel.
- Discuss what the beans will need to sprout (sunlight and, eventually, soil and water). Consult a book on growing beans, such as *Beans: All About Them*, written by Alvin and Virginia Silverstein, illustrated by Shirley Chan (Prentice-Hall, 1975).
- Chart students' estimates of how tall their beans will sprout.
- For story props, place several assorted beans in a small fabric bag. Let children take turns trading an imaginary cow (played by two students) for the magic beans.
- Spray-paint poker chips gold for coins and plastic eggs for golden eggs.

Jack and the Beanstalk
Learning Connection

J IS FOR JACK . . .
Introduce the students to words that begin with "J," such as Jack, jump, jewelry, and jelly. Have the children brainstorm as many "J" words as they can.

JACK'S WRITING ASSIGNMENT
Duplicate the writing worksheet (p. 137) and give one to each child in the class. Have the children practice printing the letter "J" and words that begin with "J" by copying the examples given or using words chosen from the class' brainstormed list.

JACK'S FOLDER
Duplicate the folder cover (p. 138) and give one to each child to color and glue to the front of a manila folder. Provide green crayons for children to use to color the beanstalk. Children can keep all the work from this unit in their folder.

Jack

jelly

J j

J j

137

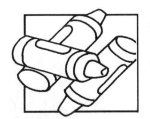

Jack and the Beanstalk
Art Connection

PAPER BAG GIANTS

Materials:
Brown paper bags (two per child), newspaper, crayons, construction paper, scissors, glue or paste, tape, green crepe-paper streamers

Directions:
1. Have the children draw a giant's face on one of their bags. They can also cut facial features from construction paper and glue or paste the cutouts to the bag. (Note: Have the children turn the bag so that the opening points down.)
2. Have the children draw (or cut and paste) clothing on the other bag. (Note: Make sure that on this section, the bag opening points up.)
3. Provide newspaper for the children to crumple and stuff into the bags.
4. Show children how to tape the top bag over the bottom bag, with the edges overlapping slightly.
5. Display these paper bag giants along one wall of the classroom, underneath a green, crepe-paper streamer "beanstalk" border.

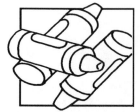

Jack and the Beanstalk
Art Connection

A BEVY OF BEANSTALKS

BEANSTALK 1

Materials:
Garden poles, green Styrofoam sheet, green yarn

Directions:
1. Stick a package of garden poles randomly into a thick sheet of green Styrofoam.
2. Let several students at a time wrap balls of green yarn around the poles to make beanstalks.

BEANSTALK 2

Materials:
White paper, crayons, markers, glue, green glitter and sequins, green tempera paint, paintbrushes, scissors, green crepe paper, pushpins

Directions:
1. Draw a simple leaf pattern onto white paper, duplicate, and give one to each child to color and cut out.
2. Provide a variety of decorations for children to use to beautify their leaves.
3. Help children write their names on their leaves.
4. Pin a long piece of green crepe paper down one wall.
5. Post the children's leaves up and down the crepe paper stem to make the beanstalk.

Jack and the Beanstalk
Discovery Connection

MAGIC BEANS

Materials:
Plastic dishpan, assorted dried beans (kidney, lima, garbanzo, navy), plastic containers, measuring cups, measuring spoons, kitchen scale, paper, marker, water

Directions:
1. Pour an assortment of beans in plastic containers at the manipulatives table.
2. Set out a plastic dishpan, measuring cups, spoons, and a kitchen scale near the beans.
3. Have the children experiment measuring and weighing the assorted beans. When they pour the beans, encourage them to pour over the plastic dishpan (to catch stray beans).
4. Encourage the children to observe the beans in many different ways. They can try to match the same amount of kidney beans to garbanzo beans. They can submerge a few beans in water to see what happens.
5. Help the children record their experiments and results.

Option:
Have students trace around the different variety of beans on their experiment result sheets.

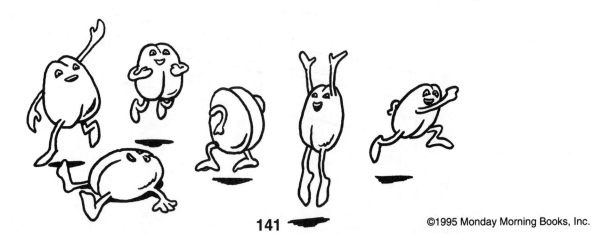

Jack and the Beanstalk
Math Connection

GOLDEN GOOSE MATH

Materials:
Goose pattern (p. 143), paper, scissors, crayons, stapler, bowl, plastic eggs (spray-painted gold) or eggs cut from stiff yellow paper

Directions:
1. Give each child a copy of the goose pattern to color.
2. Color two copies of the goose pattern yourself, cut out, and staple together at the top.
3. Place your goose pattern over a small bowl filled with the golden eggs.
4. Tell story problems as a class. For example, ask the children the following question: "If a hen laid one egg yesterday and one egg to-day, how many eggs would she have laid?" Pull the eggs out of the bowl as you work through the problems.

Jack and the Beanstalk
Snack Connection

GIANT FOOD!

Ingredients:
A variety of different-sized foods (see below), salad dressing

Directions:
1. Bring in an assortment of big and little vegetables. You might find baby carrots and normal-sized carrots, huge baking potatoes and tiny red potatoes, cherry tomatoes and hot-house tomatoes, large ears of corn and the tiny variety.
2. Let children observe the different-sized food (fare fit for a giant) before nibbling on the various vegetable snacks. Serve the vegetables with different dips.

Option:
Also offer other different-sized snacks including mini- and regular-sized crackers, pretzels, juice boxes (which come in "junior" size), and cookies.

WE'VE BEEN EATING BEANS!
- Make cans of bean and bacon soup. Serve with croutons.
- Heat cans of baked beans and serve with melted cheese.
- Serve refried bean dip (hot or cold) with cut vegetable sticks or tortilla chips.
- Make three (or four) bean salad from green beans, wax beans, kidney beans, and garbanzo beans. Add a simple oil and vinegar dressing.

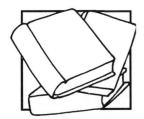

Jack and the Beanstalk
Resources

David's Father by Robert Munsch (Annick Press, 1983).
Julie tries to get over her apprehension of her friend David's father, who happens to be a giant, in this humorously illustrated story.

The Giant's Toe by Brock Cole (Farrar, 1986).
This delightful take-off on Jack and the Beanstalk features a lovable giant and an impish "toe." Text of varying length on each page.

The Good Giants and the Bad Pukwudgies by Jean Fritz, illustrated by Tomie de Paola (Putnam's, 1982).
Fritz tells how the geography of Cape Cod was formed by a giant and his family during battles with the pukwudgies as recounted by Wampanoag legend.

The History of Mother Twaddle and the Marvelous Achievements of Her Son Jack by Paul Galdone (Seabury Press, 1974).
A humorous and lively version of Jack and the Beanstalk.

Idle Jack by Anthony Maitland (Farrar, Strauss, 1977).
Humorous rendition with a focus on the days of the week.

Jack and the Beanstalk by Matt Faulkner (Scholastic, 1986).
Short text for the beginning reader accompanies pastel illustrations.

Jack and the Beanstalk by John Howe (Little, Brown, 1989).
Splendidly illustrated version.

Jack and the Beanstalk by Steven Kellogg (Lucky Book Club, Scholastic, 1965).
Illustrations are predominantly black and white with green additions.

Jack and the Beanstalk by William Stobbs (Delacorte Press, 1965).
Three color illustrations with long, long text.

Jack and the Bean Tree, A Mountain Tale Retold by Gail E. Haley (Crown, 1986).
Unique illustrations and regional vocabulary.

Jack and the Fire Dragon by Gail Haley (Crown, 1988).
Jack encounters a menacing monster (Fire Dragon) and then rescues three sisters in this story. Vibrant illustrations seem to jump off the page.

Jack and the Giant Killer: Jack's First and Finest Adventure Retold in Verse as Well as Other Useful Information About Giants by Beatrice de Regniers (Atheneum, 1987).
Retells in verse Jack's encounter with a giant, including such lore as the right way to shake hands with a giant. Whimsically detailed art and short text make this a must for the early childhood classroom.

Jack and the Beanstalk
Resources

Jack and the Whoopie Wind by Mary Calhoun, illustrated by Dick Gackenbach (William Morrow, 1987). Humorous illustrations depict an angry Jack. He is mad at the wind for blowing everything away, so he tries a succession of ways to stop it.

The Jack Tales: Told by R.M. Ward and His Kin by Richard Chase (Houghton Mifflin, 1943).
Two hundred and two pages of "Jack" stories and history. This is a great resource for teachers to expand their repertoire of "Jack" lore.

Jim and the Beanstalk by Raymond Briggs (Coward McCann, 1970).
In this version, Jack helps the giant get glasses, false teeth, and a wig and then is rewarded with a piece of the giant's gold.

Ladder to the Sky: A Legend Retold by Barbara Juster Esbenssen (Little, Brown, 1989).
This folktale recounts how the gift of healing came to the Ojibway people. Vines are the ladder to the sky in this book of beautiful illustrations and intricate borders.

Mickey and the Beanstalk by the Walt Disney Co. (Random House, 1973).
Cute illustrations interspersed with short text.

Sing Me a Story by Jane Browne (Crown, 1991).
Features thirteen songs based on well-known nursery rhymes and fairy tales. Instructions for making action movements accompany each song.

OTHER
Jack and the Beanstalk (CBS/Fox Video, 1983).
This video is in the Faerie Tale Theatre series, and stars Dennis Christopher, Elliott Gould, Jean Stapleton, and Katherine Helmond.

Jack and the Beanstalk Collection read by Robby Benson (Durkin Hayes, 1994).
This cassette is in the "Classic Tales" series.

Jack and the Beanstalk (Worldvision Home Video, 1985).
This magical blend of live action and animation was produced and directed by Gene Kelly, with original songs by Sammy Cahn and James Van Heusen.

Jack and the Beanstalk (UNI Distribution, 1991).
This Rabbit Ears Production of the classic British tale is narrated by Michael Palin, with music by David Stewart and illustrations by Ed Sorel.

Kings

STORY SUMMARY

Kings are very important characters in fairy tales and nursery rhymes. There's Old King Cole (a merry old soul), and greedy King Midas (with the golden touch). There's the king in the counting house (counting all his money), and the King of Hearts (a chef, no less, who baked his queen a treat). There are many kings who don't have names, but who play important parental roles to famous princesses in fairy tales. Ask your students to brainstorm as many kings as they can!

SETTING THE STAGE: KING FOR A DAY

Materials:

Writing paper, white paper, matches, marker, gold paper, gold spray paint, scissors, paper plate, plastic utensils, plastic foods, paper cup

Directions:

- Discuss the names of kings that the students might be familiar with from stories. Write the names down on a royal chart (a piece of paper cut into a crown shape).
- Discuss the attributes that make a king a good ruler.
- Singe the edges of dampened writing paper with a flame to give it an antique look. Write down the students' royal edicts and proclamations and post them on a regal bulletin board, bordered with gold paper.
- Spray-paint gold a cup, plate, plastic foods, and plastic silverware to show items that King Midas touched. Read *King Midas* by Catherine Storr (Raintree, 1985), and then bring out the "gold" items.

147

Kings
Learning Connection

K IS FOR KINGS . . .

Introduce your students to words that begin with "K," such as king-dom, kite, and kind. Have the children brainstorm as many "K" words as they can. Depending on the age of your children, you might also want to discuss words that are spelled differently but sound the same, such as "knight" and "night," and words that start with silent "K's," such as "knife" and "knees."

KING'S WRITING ASSIGNMENT

Duplicate the writing worksheet (p. 149) and give one to each child in the class. Have the children practice printing the letter "K" and words that begin with "K" by copying the examples given or choosing words from the brainstormed vocabulary list.

KING'S FOLDER

Duplicate the folder cover (p. 150) and give one to each child to color and glue to the front of a manila folder. Provide gold watercolors or glue and gold glitter for children to use to decorate the crown. They can also glue on sequin "jewels." Children can keep all the work from this unit in their folder.

King

kite

K

k

149

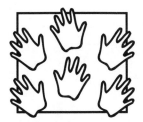

Kings
Learning Connection

MOTHER GOOSE—FIT FOR A KING!
Your students will be sure to love these Mother Goose rhymes. Read them at story time, or while children are decorating their crowns.

LAVENDER'S BLUE
Lavender's blue, diddle, diddle,
Lavender's green;
When I am king, diddle, diddle,
You shall be queen.

LITTLE KING PIPPIN
Little King Pippin he built a fine hall,
Pie-crust and pastry-crust that was the
    wall;
The windows were made of black pud-
    ding and white,
And slated with pancakes, you ne'er
    saw the like!

OLD KING COLE
Old King Cole
Was a merry old soul,
And a merry old soul was he;
He called for his pipe,
And he called for his bowl,
And he called for his fiddlers three.

Every fiddler, he had a fine fiddle,
And a very fine fiddle had he;
Twee tweedle dee, tweedle dee, went
    the fiddlers.
Oh, there's none so rare
As can compare
With King Cole and his fiddlers three.

A RAINBOW
Purple, yellow, red and green,
The King cannot reach it nor the
    Queen;
Nor can the wise man, whose power is
    great:
Tell me this riddle while I count eight!

FOR WANT OF A NAIL
For want of a nail, the shoe was lost,
For want of a shoe, the horse was lost,
For want of a horse, the rider was lost,
For want of a rider, the battle was lost,
For want of a battle the kingdom was
    lost,
And all for the want of a horseshoe nail!

THE KING OF FRANCE
The King of France went up the hill
With forty thousand men;
The King of France came down the hill,
And ne'er went up again.

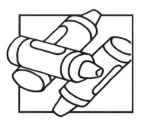

Kings
Art Connection

CROWNS FOR KINGS (AND QUEENS, TOO)
Paper crowns make great props for future kings and queens to wear.

Materials:
Large sheets of construction paper in a variety of colors, scissors, tape, glitter, glue, sequins, markers, stickers

Directions:
1. Let each child choose a color of construction paper to make a crown.
2. Show students how to cut jagged edges along the top of their papers but to leave the rest alone.
3. Provide sequins, stickers, and markers for children to use to decorate their crowns.
4. Help children size their crowns and tape the edges together to make them easy to slip on and off.
5. Let the children wear their crowns during a parade around the classroom, or while you read Mother Goose poems (p. 151).

CASTLE ART

Materials:
Black construction paper, scissors, gold and silver watercolors, paintbrushes, white paper, marker, gold and silver glitter, glue, easels

Directions:
1. At the paint easels, post black construction paper cut in "royal" shapes, for example, large crowns, round gold pieces, simple thrones.
2. Provide gold and silver paint, brushes, glitter, and glue for children to use to make artwork fit for a castle.
3. Hang these on a wall in the "King's Art Gallery."

Kings
Math Connection

MONEY MATH

Materials:
Play money or penny rolls, index card box spray-painted gold

Directions:
1. Let children take turns counting out their money (in their counting houses).
2. Ask math questions that suit the ability of your children. For example, have the kings and queens line up columns of ten pennies. Have them add the lines together, or subtract one line from another.

Note: Use oversized play money for the younger classes. For students old enough not to put money in their mouths, use pennies in rolls.

Kings
Discovery Connection

OLD KING COLE'S PIPES

Materials:
Bubble pipes or straws, bubble solution, water table

Directions:
1. At the water table, place bubble pipes and bubble solution. (Note: The favor section of many stationery, toy, or party stores sell these in bulk.) You can also use straws.
2. Let children pretend to be Old King Cole, and call for their pipes.
3. They can use their pipes (or straws) to blow beautiful bubbles. (Note: Remind students to only blow and not suck on their pipes!)

Option:
Set out large dishpans of bubble solution along with large bubble wands. Children will need to share these plastic wands, but they are fairly inexpensive at toy or science stores.

Bubble Resources:
- *The Unbelievable Bubble Book* by John Cassidy with David Stein (inventor of "The Bubble Thing") (Klutz Press, 1991). This great resource includes information on bubbles, tricks, and the very best recipes for making bubbles.
- The Bubble Thing ($8 plus $2 shipping). Klutz Press, 2121 Stauton Ct., Palo Alto, CA 94306.
- *Kids Discover: Bubbles* (April, 1992). This issue of the magazine is completely on bubbles. Order from Kids Discover, 170 Fifth Avenue, New York, NY 10010. (1-24 copies are $3 each. 25+ copies are $1.25 each.)

Kings
Discovery Connection

BATHING KING BIDGOOD

Read *King Bidgood's in the Bathtub* by Audrey Wood, illustrated by Don Wood (Harcourt, 1985) before doing this activity. In this story, the page is frustrated when the king decides to spend all day in the bathtub. None of the court folk are able to remove the king from his sudsy haven, but the resourceful page finally solves the problem himself.

Materials:
Plastic baby doll, baby bathtub or plastic dishpan

Directions:
1. Put a plastic baby doll in a baby bathtub.
2. Ask children to help you choose a variety of items to put in the tub with "King Bidgood."
3. Pretend that the pretend King Bidgood doesn't want to get out of the tub. Ask the refrain from the book, "Oh, who knows what to do?" (The students will surely think up answers!)

Option:
Use this activity to discuss the proper way to take care of babies. If any of your students have new baby brothers or sisters, find out if a parent is available to bring in the new baby. Discuss bathing, feeding, sleeping, and so on.

Kings
Snack Connection

KING BIDGOOD'S BLUE BUBBLES

Ingredients:
Blue Jell-O, whipped cream, clear plastic cups

Directions:
1. In clear plastic cups, make individual servings of blue Jell-O according to the directions on the package.
2. Dot the top of each serving with whipped cream (for bubbles).

COUNTING COINS

Ingredients:
Gold foil-covered chocolate coins

Directions:
1. Serve chocolate coins in their gold covers.
2. Let students count their coins before snack time.

Kings
Resources

BOOKS

The Amazing Pig by Paul Galdone (Clarion, 1981).
An old Hungarian tale is retold by Galdone.

The King at the Door by Brock Cole (Doubleday, 1979).
A king pays a visit at the local inn, but only the young boy takes him at his word that he is indeed the king. In the end, the lad is rewarded. Short text with color illustrations alternating with black and white.

King Bidgood's in the Bathtub by Audrey Wood, illustrated by Don Wood (Harcourt, 1985).
This Caldecott Honor Book has excellent illustrations. Despite pleas from his court, a fun-loving king refuses to get out of his bathtub and rule his kingdom.

King Gorboduc's Fabulous Zoo by Stephen Boswell (Dutton, 1986).
The zoo keeper and the jester (with the help of the animals) devise a plan to set the animals free. Animals include a dodo, griffin, woolly mammoth, dragon, and unicorn.

The King Has Horse's Ears by Peggy Thomson, illustrated by David Small (Simon and Schuster, 1988).
Only the king and his barber know that the king has horse's ears until the secret gets out—just in time for the king's wedding day.

King Henry's Palace by Pat Hutchins (Greenwillow, 1983).
Three short stories about a pleasant palace where a nice king lives happily with his cook, gardener, servants, and guards, who wish only to please him.

King Krakus and the Dragon by Janina Domanska (Greenwillow, 1979).
In this story, the townspeople are terrified by a dragon until the shoemaker's apprentice devises a plan to rid the town of the monster.

King Midas by Catherine Storr (Raintree, 1985).
This version features large colorful paintings with short text.

King Midas Has a Gilt Complex by Roy Doty (Doubleday, 1979).
This is an illustrated collection of jokes, riddles, puns, and gags that children will love!

King of the Birds by Shirley Climo, illustrated by Ruth Heller (Crowell, 1988).
Chaos reigns among the birds, until a contest is held to see who will be King of the Birds.

King of the Cats by Paul Galdone (Clarion, 1980).
Old Tom, the family pet, listens intently as the grave digger tells his wife how a band of cats marched into the cemetery to mourn their dead king.

King Wacky by Dick Gackenback (Crown, 1984).
King Wacky, born with his head on backwards, proceeds to do everything in a backward way.

The King Who Rained by Fred Gwynne (Simon and Schuster, 1970).
A little girl pictures the things her parents talk about, such as a king who rained, bear feet, and the foot prince in the snow.

The King's Chessboard by David Birch (Dial, 1988).
A proud king, too vain to admit what he does not know, learns a valuable lesson when he grants his wise man a special request.

Kings
Resources

The King's Flower by Mitsumasa Anno (Philomel, 1976).
Larger-than-life illustrations truly bring home the point as the king discovers that bigger is not always better.

The King's Fountain by Lloyd Alexander, illustrated by Ezra Jack Keats (Dutton, 1971).
This is a powerful tale about a poor, simple man who does what others will not do, in order to help his family and neighbors.

The King's Stilts by Dr. Seuss (Random House, 1939).
The king wears his stilts every day after work, until they are stolen by a wicked man. Eric, his page boy, finally recovers the stilts. Fun pictures but the text is lengthy.

The King's Toothache by Colin West (Lippincot, 1987).
Unable to find a dentist for the king's toothache, Nurse Mary tries a baker, a town crier, and a sailor before the poor man gets relief. Large print text accents colorful, finely detailed illustrations.

Of Cobblers and Kings by Aby Aure Sheldon (Parents, 1978).
Because of his common sense, a clever cobbler rises from one important post to another until he becomes the grand chancellor of the kingdom. This book features colorful cartoon illustrations and short text.

Our King Has Horns by Richard Pevear (Macmillan, 1987).
A young barber discovers the king's horns while cutting his hair. The barber is sworn to secrecy or he will lose his life.

Princess Furball by Charlotte Huck (Greenwillow, 1989).
In a variation of Cinderella, a princess in a coat of a thousand furs hides her identity from a king who falls in love with her.

The Riddle by Adele Vernon, illustrated by Robert Rayevsky and Vladimar Radunsky (Dodd, Mead, 1987).
A retelling of a traditional Catalan tale in which a poor charcoal maker's cleverness wins him an unexpected fortune.

17 Kings and 42 Elephants by Margaret Mahy (Dial, 1987).
Seventeen kings and 42 elephants romp with a variety of jungle animals during their journey through a wild, wet night.

OTHER
King Midas and the Golden Touch (Rabbit Ears Productions, 1991).
Michael Caine narrates this classic tale for ages 5 and up. It also features veteran jazz pianist Ellis Marsalis and cellist Yo-Yo Ma. Illustrated by Reynold Ruffins.

Little Mermaid

STORY SUMMARY

A young mermaid falls in love with a human being. She is willing to give up her fins and her underwater life in order to acquire legs and meet her dream man. However, she has only three days to make him fall in love with her, or she will turn into silvery ocean foam.

SETTING THE STAGE: LOVELY LITTLE MERMAIDS

Materials:

Bowl of goldfish or aquarium, drawing paper, markers, games and puzzles with underwater themes, swimming fins, goggles, swimming masks

Directions:

- Enhance this underwater theme by setting a bowl of goldfish or an aquarium on a low table for children to observe. Place drawing paper and markers nearby, and encourage students to draw what they see.
- Consider a field trip to a local aquarium. (If this is possible, be sure to enlist parent volunteers to help out!)
- Set out any available games or puzzles with undersea-life themes.
- Many students may have "Little Mermaid" items (from Disney) at home. Ask them to bring these in for show and tell.
- Swimming fins make great mermaid (and mermen) props, as do swimming masks and goggles. Also ask your students to bring in any fish or mermaid Halloween costumes they have to lend to your costume corner.

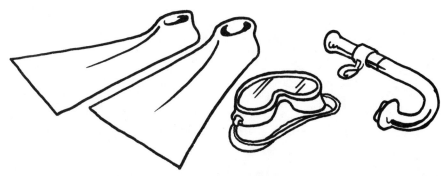

The Little Mermaid
Learning Connection

L IS FOR LITTLE . . .
Introduce the students to words that begin with "L," such as little, love, list, lights, long, and lady. Have the children brainstorm as many "L" words as they can.

THE LITTLE MERMAID'S WRITING ASSIGNMENT
Duplicate the writing worksheet (p. 161) and give one to each child in the class. Have the children practice printing the letter "L" and words that begin with "L" by copying the examples given or choosing from their long list of brainstormed words.

THE LITTLE MERMAID'S FOLDER
Duplicate the folder cover (p. 162) and give one to each child to color and glue to the front of a manila folder. Provide silver glitter and glue for children to use as foam. Gold star stickers make great starfish! Children can keep all the work from this unit in their folder.

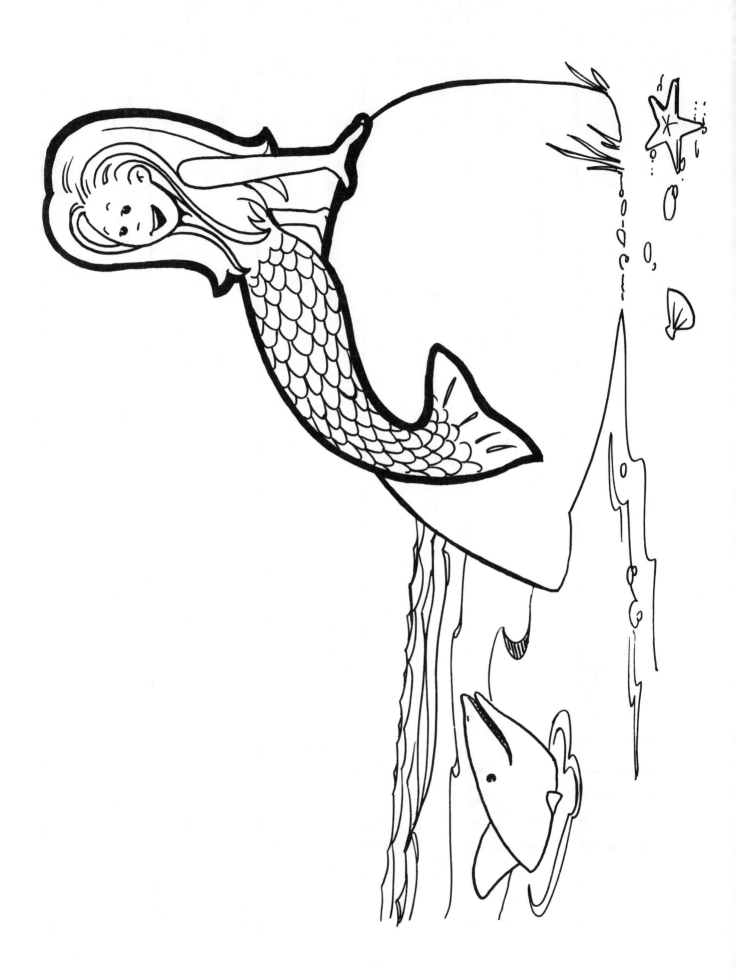

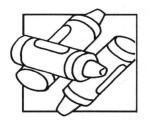

The Little Mermaid
Art Connection

BY THE SEA, BY THE BEAUTIFUL SEA

Materials:
Underwater patterns and shell pattern (p. 164), blue construction paper, shell noodles, small plastic or paper dishes, sand, squeeze bottles of glue, crayons, silver glitter, scissors

Directions:
1. On a long table, set squeeze bottles of glue and dishes of un-cooked shell noodles and sand.
2. Give each child a sheet of blue construction paper. (Have a few shades of blue to choose from.)
3. Students can dribble glue onto their papers and sprinkle it with the sand and the noodles.
4. Duplicate the underwater patterns and give a sheet to each child to color and cut out. Children can use these patterns to add to their seaside pictures.
5. Provide silver glitter for children to glue to their oceans to make sparkling waves.
6. Post the completed pictures on a "By the Beautiful Sea" bulletin board. Enlarge the shell pattern, cut out, and use it as a border.

Option:
Cover the bulletin board with blue plastic wrap.

164

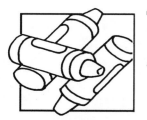

The Little Mermaid
Art Connection

LOVELY MERMAID VISORS

Materials:
Paper plates (one per child), mermaid folder pattern (p. 162), scissors, crayons, glue

Directions:
1. Cut out the rim of a paper plate for each child to use for a visor.
2. Duplicate the mermaid pattern and give one to each child to color and cut out.
3. Have students decorate the paper plate visors by gluing the patterns onto the edges.
4. Encourage the students to wear their visors in a parade of the mermaids and mermen. They can spice up their outfits with long wigs, flippers, goggles, sunglasses, and so on.

The Little Mermaid
Math Connection

SHE SORTS SEASHELLS

Materials:
Shell noodles (large and small), rubbing alcohol, food coloring, glue, construction paper, crayons or markers, waxed paper, newspaper

Directions:
1. The day before you plan on doing this activity, dye small and large shell noodles. Soak the noodles in a rubbing alcohol and food coloring solution until they reach the desired color. Air dry on waxed paper on top of newspaper. (Note: Save the dyed alcohol in the original bottles and use again and again.)
2. Give each child enough of the dyed shells to count and sort.
3. Let students make permanent patterns with their shells by gluing them onto strips of paper.
4. Have the children number the shells on their paper using crayons or markers.

The Little Mermaid
Discovery Connection

SEASIDE SCENES

Materials:
Seashells, sand table or plastic dishpan filled with sand, water table, plastic boats, plastic fish

Directions:
1. Place an assortment of shells in the sand table or in a pan of sand.
2. Encourage the children to pick up the shells and place them near their ears.
3. Ask the children to tell you what they hear. They will be interested to know that what they are listening to is actually the sound of their heartbeats!
4. Set up the water table with plastic boats and fish.
5. Encourage the children to create small waves in the water table and to maneuver their boats along the swells.
6. Have children take turns going back and forth between the two stations.

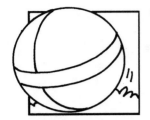

The Little Mermaid
Games Connection

SIDE STEPPING

Directions:
1. Have students spread out in the classroom (or outside) so that everyone has room.
2. Show the students how to walk like a crab. They can simply side step while standing, or use their hands and feet to move with a crabby shuffle. (See illustration.)
3. Discuss the difficulty of side stepping. Ask if the children are happy to have human legs. If they're not, have them describe the type of paws, fins, wheels, wings, etc., that they'd rather have.

The Little Mermaid
Snack Connection

A SEASIDE SMORGASBORD!
- Serve fish sticks and catsup.
- Let children help you mix up tuna salad and spread it on crackers or thinly sliced bread.
- Serve a selection of Goldfish crackers and Gummi fish.
- Sample sardines, shrimp cocktail, salmon, or sole.
- Purchase (or have donated) a whole crab and let the children enjoy a multisensory experience! Many fish markets will clean and crack the crab.

The Little Mermaid
Resources

BOOKS

It's Perfectly True and Other Stories by Hans Christian Andersen, translated from the Danish by Paul Leyssac, illustrated by Richard Bennett (Harcourt, 1931).
This book includes "The Little Mermaid," "The Princess and the Pea," "The Tinderbox," "The Ugly Duckling," "The Snow Queen," "Thumbelina," "The Wild Swans," and others.

The Little Mermaid adapted by Anthea Bell, illustrated by Chihiro Iwasaki (Picture Book Studio, 1984).
A little sea princess, longing to be human, trades her mermaid tail for legs in hopes of earning herself an immortal soul.

Michael Hague's Favourite Hans Christian Andersen Fairy Tales (Holt, Rinehart and Winston, 1981).
Includes nine favorite Andersen tales that are heavy on text and have a few full-page Hague illustrations each.

Walt Disney Presents: The Little Mermaid (Gallery Books, 1989).
A little sea princess, who wishes she were human, trades her mermaid's tail in for human legs, hoping to win the heart of the prince she loves.

OTHER

Disney's Sebastian: From The Little Mermaid (Walt Disney, 1989).
This sound recording includes one sound cassette and one sheet of lyrics from the motion picture.

The Little Mermaid (AW Audio, 1993).
This unabridged version of Hans Christian Andersen's story is narrated by Aurora Wetzel.

The Little Mermaid (Playhouse Video, 1987).
This Faerie Tale Theatre presentation tells the tale of a mermaid who falls in love with a sailor and makes a deal with a sea witch to be able to live as a woman on land.

The Little Mermaid (Walt Disney Home Video).
In this animated version of Hans Christian Andersen's classic tale, the Little Mermaid rescues a prince whose boat has capsized. She makes a deal with the sea witch in order to gain human legs.

Little Mermaid Magazines
P.O. Box 7556
Red Oak, IA 51591

Mitten

STORY SUMMARY

When a boy loses his mitten in the woods, all the woodland creatures make good use of it. One after another, they climb inside to keep warm for the winter. Unfortunately, the mitten can stretch only so much, and when too many animals climb inside the seams burst!

SETTING THE STAGE: MAGNIFICENT MITTENS

Materials:

Mittens, gloves, muffs, socks, shoes, boots, large sheet of paper, marker, scissors

Directions:

- Collect an assortment of mittens and gloves. Have students match the pairs together. Discuss when each type of item would be used to best advantage.
- This unit provides a fine opportunity for children to practice the self-help skills of getting dressed. Set out mittens, gloves, muffs, socks, shoes, and boots for children to pull on and take off.
- For language expansion, discuss cold weather vocabulary. Ask children to list all the cold weather words they can think of, and write them down on a mitten-shaped piece of paper.
- Discuss different kinds of winter animal behaviors. Ask the children to name the animals that they see in their neighborhood during wintertime.
- Have a school-wide drive to collect mittens and cold-weather items for the homeless in your community.

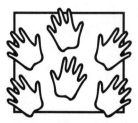

The Mitten
Learning Connection

M IS FOR MITTEN . . .
Introduce the students to words that begin with "M," such as mitten, mountain, movie, and marble. Have the children brainstorm as many "M" words as they can.

MITTEN'S WRITING ASSIGNMENT
Duplicate the writing worksheet (p. 173) and give one to each child in the class. Have the children practice printing the letter "M" and words that begin with "M" by copying the examples given or some of the marvelous words from their brainstormed vocabulary list.

MITTEN'S FOLDER
Duplicate the folder cover (p. 174) and give one to each child to color and tape to the front of a manila folder. Have the children tape only three sides closed. Duplicate the animal patterns (p. 175) for children to color and cut out. They can slide the animal cutouts into the mitten "pocket." Children can keep all the work from this unit in their folder.

Mitten

mouse

M

m

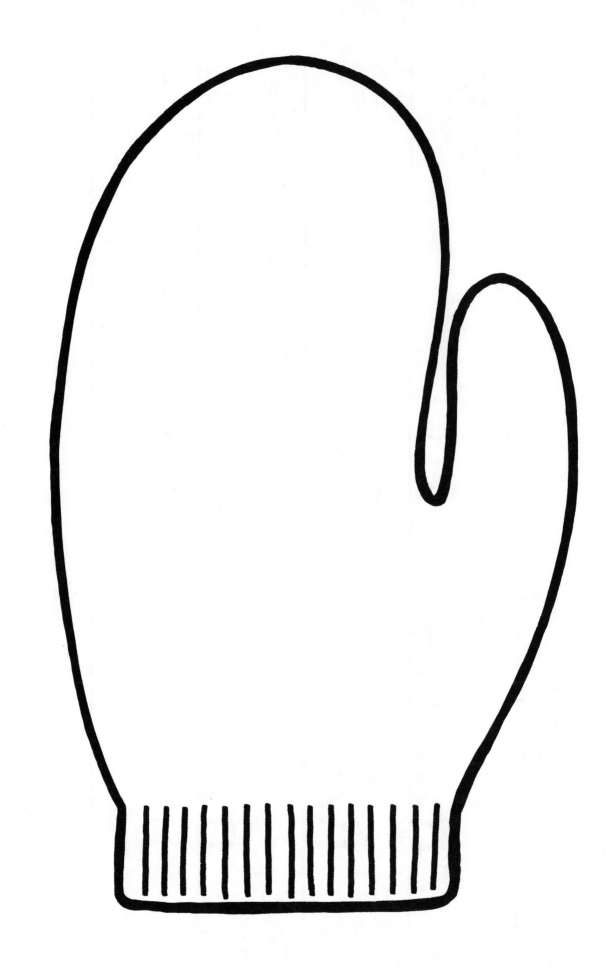

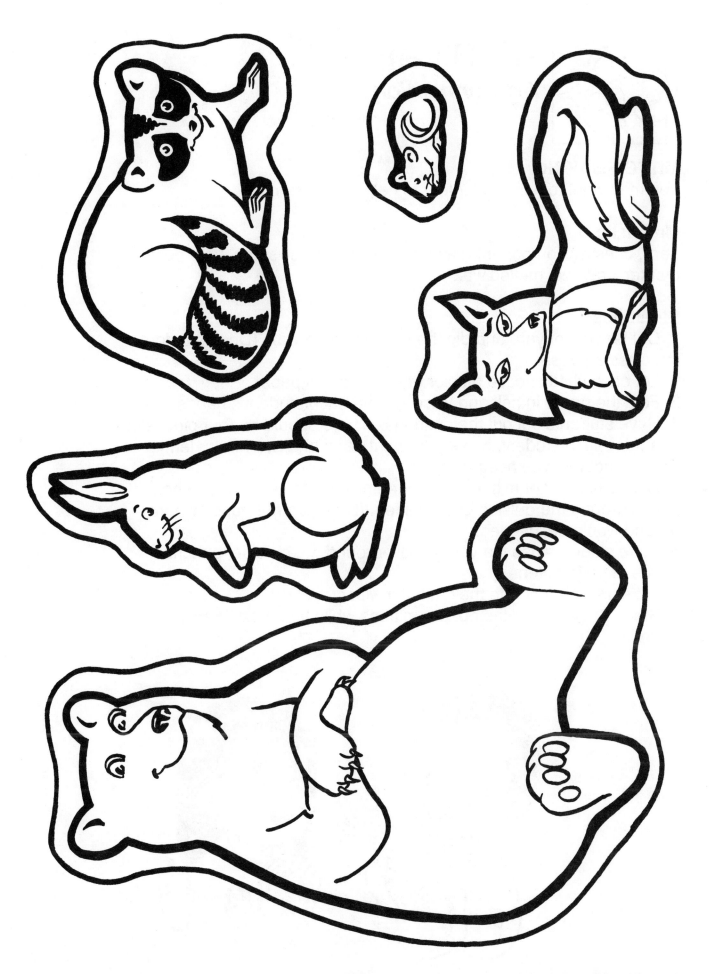

175 ©1995 Monday Morning Books, Inc.

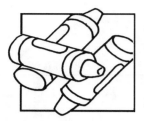

The Mitten
Art Connection

MITTEN-MAKING
You may want to ask a volunteer to help with this activity.

Materials:
Yarn, construction paper (in a variety of colors), scissors, hole punch, marker, crayons, melted wax

Directions:
1. Cut lengths of yarn and dip the tips in melted wax. (Do this before the class arrives.)
2. Let each child choose a color of construction paper.
3. Fold the paper in half and trace around each student's hands.
4. Have students cut out their mittens. (There should be four pieces of paper for each student, two for the right hand and two for the left.) Assist students who need help.
5. Hold each pair of mittens together (lining up the edges) and hole punch around the outside of the mitten. (Note: Do not punch where a hand would be inserted.)
6. Have students use the yarn to sew around the outside, punched edges of their mittens.
7. Let students decorate their mittens with crayons.
8. Students can wear their paper mittens while you read them *The Mitten*.

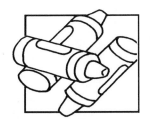

The Mitten
Art Connection

AMAZING ANIMAL MASKS
Each student can make an animal mask on a paper plate. Encourage students to make masks of the different animals that appear in the story.

Materials:
Paper plates (one per child), construction paper (in a variety of colors), scissors, glue, yarn, stapler, markers, crayons, felt scraps, buttons, pipe cleaners, sheet or large cardboard box

Directions:
1. Before doing this activity, cut out eye holes in each plate and staple a length of yarn to each edge at ear level.
2. Give each student a plate to decorate using crayons, markers, or cutouts from construction paper. For more detailed animals, provide pipe cleaners or yarn for whiskers, buttons for noses, and felt scraps for fuzzy ears.
3. Let your students put on a production of *The Mitten* while wearing their masks. Help them tie on the masks with the lengths of yarn.
4. The mitten itself can be a sheet draped over a clothesline (that the children duck under), or a cardboard box (that they climb inside). Or children can just use their imaginations!

The Mitten
Math Connection

PAIRING OFF

Directions:
1. Have students practice counting by twos throughout the day.
2. Encourage them to look for things that come in pairs, for example, eyes, shoes, pants, legs, mittens.
3. As children name different kinds of pairs, chart their ideas on a large sheet of paper.

Option 1:
Make pattern pairs for children to count. (They can also use the patterns to play a game of Concentration.) Duplicate the animal patterns (p. 175; make two copies), or draw and cut out pairs of mittens, gloves, shoes, and so on.

Option 2:
As you chart things that come in twos, talk about even numbers.

Option 3:
Create and work story problems with creatures and mittens. Then ask your children how many mittens six children would need. Lead up to how many mittens your entire class would need.

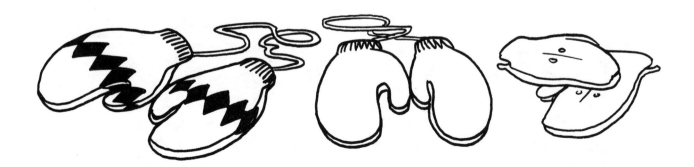

The Mitten
Discovery Connection

MITTEN MANIPULATIVES

Materials:
Styrofoam packing peanuts or air-popped popcorn, dishpan (or manipulatives table), assorted plastic or wooden animals, assorted mittens

Directions:
1. Place Styrofoam peanuts or air-popped popcorn in a dishpan for snow.
2. Place an assortment of tiny plastic or wooden animals in the "snow."
3. Add some mittens in a variety of colors. (Save the single mittens that wind up in your "Lost and Found" at the end of each winter for this project.)
4. Have students retell the story of *The Mitten* as they play with the manipulatives.

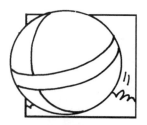

The Mitten
Games Connection

MARVELOUS MITTEN

Materials:
Old sheet or large piece of felt, scissors, thick yarn and needle (or sewing machine), stuffed animals (optional)

Directions:
1. Cut out a huge mitten from an old sheet or a large piece of felt.
2. Sew the lower outside edges shut with thick yarn or sew an outside seam on a sewing machine.
3. Depending on the size of the mitten, students can deposit stuffed animals into the mitten, or pretend that they are the animals and climb in themselves.

Option:
Make sequence cards of the various animals from your version of the story as a prompt for younger students. Copy the animal patterns (p. 175) onto heavy paper. Line up stuffed animals, and have the children pick them up in the right order.

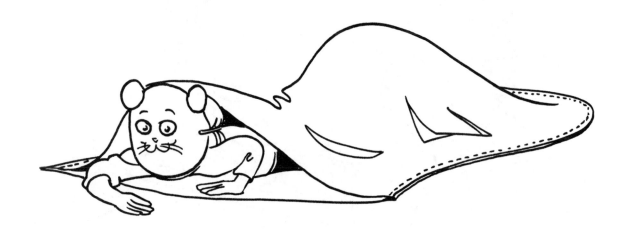

The Mitten
Snack Connection

MITTENS AND KITTENS, OH ME, OH MY!

Ingredients:
Bread, cheese slices, luncheon meat, cookie cutters (mitten- and animal-shaped, if possible)

Directions:
1. Provide bread, cheese, and luncheon meat for students to cut into pairs of shapes using cookie cutters.
2. You can combine this snack with a story problem activity. For example, cut three kittens and ask the children how many mittens the kittens would need.

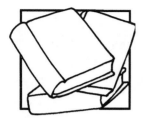

The Mitten
Resources

BOOKS

The Jacket I Wear in the Snow by Shirley Neitzel (Scholastic, 1989). The cumulative text humorously depicts a child getting dressed in layers of clothes for snow play. Rebus pictures are included in the brief text to help students "read" the story on their own.

The Mitten by Alvin Tresselt (Lothrop, Lee and Shepard, 1964). This version, adapted from E. Rachev's version, features one paragraph of text per double-page illustration in a unique style with an ethnic flavor.

The Mitten: A Ukranian Folktale by Jan Brett (Putnam's, 1989). Several animals sleep snuggly in Nicki's lost mitten until the bear sneezes. The version features a short text and gorgeous borders with their own tale around lovely Brett illustrations.

Runaway Mittens by Jean Rogers, illustrated by Rie Munoz (Greenwillow, 1988). Pica has some fine red mittens his grandmother knit for him. However, they're always showing up in strange places, and Pica can never find them when he needs them. One day Pica discovers his mittens keeping the newborn puppies warm in their box, so he leaves his mittens there.

Three Little Kittens by Paul Galdone (Clarion, 1986). Very large type and humorous illustrations depict three little kittens losing, soiling, and washing their mittens.

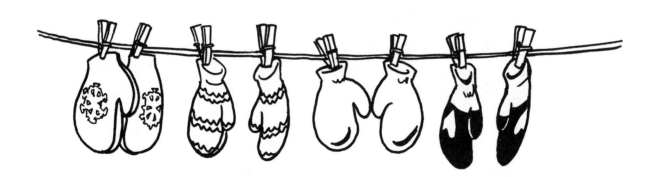

Never–Never Land

STORY SUMMARY

In J. M. Barrie's *Peter Pan*, Wendy Darling captures the shadow of the elusive Peter Pan and holds it hostage. When Peter comes looking for it, Wendy sews it back on for him. He declares to the Darling children, "I won't grow up!" and invites the three siblings on an adventure to Never Land where they meet pirates, a princess, the Lost Boys, and (of course) a pixie named Tinkerbell—all before returning to their beds in the nursery.

SETTING THE STAGE: NEVER–NEVER LAND

Materials:

Writing paper, pencil, baby powder or gold star confetti

Directions:

- Adjust the overhead lighting so the students can throw their shadows on the classroom wall. You can also take the children outside to see their shadows.
- Have students pair up and take turns seeing the other's shadow.
- Take dictation stories from the students. Ask if they would like to fly to Never Land. If so, ask if they'd want to stay or come home again.
- Play Tinkerbell and sprinkle "pixie dust" on the children. Use baby powder (which has a nice scent) or gold star confetti (which is available at costume and display stores).
- Discuss "wonderful thoughts"—which helped the Darlings learn to fly. This is an excellent time to talk about the power of positive thinking.

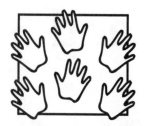

Never–Never Land
Learning Connection

N IS FOR NEVER LAND . . .
Introduce the students to words that begin with "N," such as Nana, nursery, naughty, and nice. Have the children brainstorm as many "N" words as they can.

NANA'S WRITING ASSIGNMENT
Duplicate the writing worksheet (p. 185) and give one to each child in the class. Have the children practice printing the letter "N" and words that begin with "N" by copying the examples given or choosing from their list of brainstormed words.

NEVER LAND'S FOLDER
Duplicate the folder cover (p. 186) and give one to each child to color and glue to the front of a manila folder. Provide cotton balls for children to glue on as clouds in the night sky. Gold star stickers add flair to the pictures. Children can keep all the work from this unit in their folder.

Nana

nice

N

n

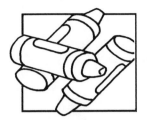

Never–Never Land
Art Connection

I WON'T GROW UP!

Materials:
Photographs of the children, drawing paper, crayons or markers, scissors, glue or tape

Directions:
1. Ask the children to bring a photo of themselves to school. (These photos will be cut apart, so make sure they are not originals.)
2. Have the children cut out their head from the photo and tape or glue it to a piece of paper.
3. Let the students draw bodies to fit their heads. Have them think about whether they want to grow up or not. If they do, have them draw on an adult body. If they don't, have them draw a body of how they'd look if they lived in Never Land.
4. Post the completed pictures on a "Peter Pan" bulletin board.

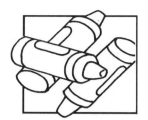

Never–Never Land
Art Connection

PETER PAN PUPPETS

Materials:
Puppet patterns (p. 189), tagboard or oak tag, scissors, markers, crayons, tempera paint, paintbrushes, straws or Popsicle sticks, glue or tape, cardboard box

Directions:
1. Duplicate the puppet patterns onto tagboard or oak tag for the children to color and cut out.
2. Provide straws or Popsicle sticks for the children to tape to the back of their puppets to use for handles.
3. Let children make a puppet theater from a cardboard box. They can decorate the theater using tempera paints.
4. Encourage children to put on a show, retelling the story of Peter Pan or creating new adventures for him using the puppets and other props.

Option:
Use the puppet patterns to make felt patterns for a felt board. Retell the story using these props. Encourage children to help you tell the story.

189

Never–Never Land
Math Connection

BY HOOK OR BY CROOK!

Materials:
Hooks (in various shapes, sizes, and colors)

Directions:
1. Collect different-sized hooks at a hardware store.
2. Let students examine the hooks, and discuss their purposes.
3. Have students sort the hooks by size, color, and type.
4. Discuss Captain Hook's hook, and why it might be useful to have a hook instead of a hand. Ask the children to think of other tools they might like to have as body parts. For example, ask if it would be useful to have wheels instead of feet, or magnets instead of fingers.

Option:
Have children draw pictures of themselves with their unique body parts.

Never–Never Land
Discovery Connection

COMPARING COMPASSES

Materials:
Compasses

Directions:
1. Bring in a few compasses for children to experiment with.
2. Have them try to read which way the compass is pointing.
3. Let the children try to navigate with a compass.

Option:
Using the treasure map made on p. 192, challenge students to use their compasses to chart their voyage from landmark to landmark.

Never–Never Land
Discovery Connection

TREASURE MAP

Materials:
Paper, crayons, prize

Directions:
1. Draw a map of the classroom and designate specific places as the locations in Never Land. For example, the water table could be the lagoon or Captain Hook's hideaway, the book corner could be the home of the Lost Boys, and so on.
2. Give clues, such as, "Walk three steps past Captain Hook's hideaway and turn left. Look under the book that's nearest to the window." Lead the students from one clue to another. (For younger children, give picture clues.)
3. Hide a treasure in some part of the room, and give children clues on how to find it. Make sure that they work together!

Treasure Idea:
Wrap a watermelon in silver foil. When the children find it, cut it open and serve it for a snack!

Never–Never Land
Snack Connection

CROCODILE SMILES

Ingredients:
Canned biscuit dough (refrigerator section), raisins

Directions:
1. Let each child mold a crocodile from canned biscuit dough.
2. The children can use raisins for eyes and small bits of dough for teeth.
3. Bake according to the directions on the package.
4. Remind the children to "Never smile at a crocodile!"

Option:
Teach the children this song:

DID YOU EVER SMILE?
(to the tune of "Do Your Ears Hang Low?")

> Did you ever smile
> At a hungry crocodile?
> Or say, "Hey, I'll see you later,"
> To a growling alligator.
> You would find it worth your while,
> To avoid the crocodile.
> Did you ever smile?

Never–Never Land
Resources

BOOKS

Nice or Nasty: A Book of Opposites by Nick Butterworth and Mick Inkpen (Little, Brown, 1987).
In large colorful illustrations with a partial line of text below, animal and human characters introduce opposite concepts.

Peter Pan by J. M. Barrie (Scribner's, 1950).
This is the original story about the adventures of the boy who would not grow up. It is too long for most young audiences to listen to attentively, but it could be read in chapters.

Peter Pan by J. M. Barrie, illustrated by Scott Gustafson (Viking, 1991).
This version is divided into seventeen chapters with fifty illustrations and beautiful maps inside the front covers. Read selected chapters to your students.

Walt Disney's Peter Pan by Bradley Coco (Western, 1989).
Concise version of the Disney movie with illustrations from the same by Ron Dias.

Walt Disney's Peter Pan and Tinker Bell and the Pirates (Golden Books, 1986).
A short segment from the story line has been elaborated upon with characters from the Disney movie.

Walt Disney's Peter Pan and Wendy by Annie North Bedford (Golden Press, 1952).
Short text and adorable illustrations.

OTHER

Peter Pan sound recording (Columbia, 1988).
Leonard Bernstein's version includes "The Darling Family at Home," "The Lost Boys," "The Pirate Song," and more.

Story of Peter Pan unabridged narration (Recorded Books, 1991).
This is a five-cassette (6.5 hour) recording.

Peter Pan Original Broadway Cast Recording (RCA, 1988).
Mary Martin, Cyril Ritchard, and others are accompanied by a chorus and orchestra.

Peter Pan (Walt Disney Home Video).
Check out the Walt Disney animated version from your local video store or library.

Old Lady Who Swallowed a Fly

STORY SUMMARY
A very (*very*) hungry old woman has a fly for an appetizer and chases it down with a spider, a bird, a cat, a dog, a goat, and a cow. She continues to swallow animals until she devours a horse. (She dies, of course!)

SETTING THE STAGE: THE OLD LADY'S LUNCH BUFFET

Materials:
Small plastic jar, miniature plastic animals, felt board, felt, animal patterns (p. 200), old lady pattern from folder cover (p. 198), scissors, crayons or markers, tape or record of "I Know an Old Lady . . ."

Directions:
- In a small plastic jar, place an assortment of miniature pigs, horses, goats, dogs, cats, cows, spiders, and flies. As students turn the jar, have them identify the various characters from the story.
- Invite some grandparents or senior friends to the school. Many seniors have musical talents that they are more than willing to share with a group of children.
- Have students enact the song as they listen to a tape or record of it, such as the classic version on *The Best of Burl Ives* (MCA, 1981). Encourage dramatic renditions of the silly song.
- Make a felt board. Color and cut out the patterns and attach a bit of felt to the back of each one. Let children help you retell the story. If possible, have the children assist in placing the animals on the felt board.

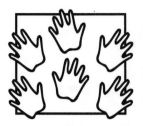

I Know an Old Lady
Who Swallowed a Fly
Learning Connection

O IS FOR OLD . . .
Introduce the students to words that begin with "O," such as old, over, orange, and odd. Have the children brainstorm as many "O" words as they can.

OLD LADY'S WRITING ASSIGNMENT
Duplicate the writing worksheet (p. 197) and give one to each child in the class. Have the children practice printing the letter "O" and words that begin with "O" by copying the examples given or by copying words from the outrageous list of brainstormed words.

OLD LADY'S FOLDER
Duplicate the folder cover (p. 198) and give one to each child to color and glue to the front of a manila folder. Duplicate and cut out the animal patterns (p. 200) for children to color and glue around the old lady pattern. Children can keep all the work from this unit in their folder.

Option:
Let the students make unique folders by stamping the fronts with insect and animal rubber stamps or by pressing on stickers.

Old

orange

O

o

197

I Know an Old Lady
Who Swallowed a Fly
Art Connection

OLD LADIES

Materials:
Old lady folder pattern (p. 198), cut-out animal patterns (p. 200), scissors, crayons, small plastic sandwich bag for each child, tape

Directions:
1. Give each child one of each animal pattern to color.
2. Help the children cut out the tummy of the old lady.
3. Show the children how to tape the plastic bag behind the old woman.
4. Let the students take turns retelling the tale to each other. They can put the animals into the old woman's tummy as the story progresses.

Option 1:
Students can color the pictures and place them in order on index cards. Help them staple the cards together to make books.

Option 2:
Help children make mobiles from the patterns. Duplicate and cut out the animal patterns onto tagboard for children to color. Punch a hole in the top of each pattern and thread a length of yarn through the hole. Tie the patterns to a hanger or a stick. Hang the mobiles in the classroom, from the ceiling or from a length of clothesline strung across the room.

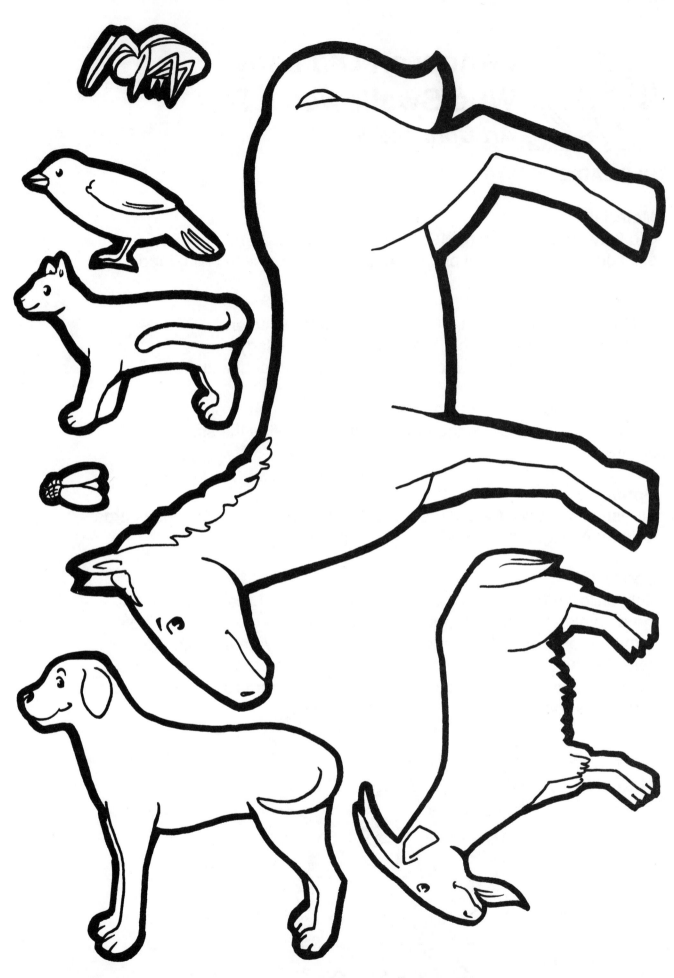

I Know an Old Lady Who Swallowed a Fly
Math Connection

YUMMY MATH

Directions:
1. Depending on the age of your students, do story problems with the characters from the story. For example, ask students how many things the old lady ate so far if she ate one fly, one spider, and one cat. If she had two insects for breakfast and three animals for lunch, a goat for a snack, and a horse and a cow for dinner, how many things did she eat that day?
2. Demonstrate the written equation for each problem.

Note: Assign younger children roles in each math problem so that they can see the equation in action.

Option 1:
Manipulatives will greatly enhance this activity.

Option 2:
Extend this activity by giving each student a paper plate. Have the children draw on the plate the foods they have eaten so far that day, then help them to add up the items. Write their number equations on slips of paper to glue to the plates. If your students enjoy this activity, they may wish to use another plate to draw imaginary things to eat and make up further equations.

I Know an Old Lady
Who Swallowed a Fly
Discovery Connection

WEIRD SCIENCE

Materials:
Plastic and wooden animals, doll, hay (optional)

Directions:
1. Put plastic or wooden farm animals on the manipulatives table with a small layer of hay covering the bottom.
2. Let children reenact the story using the plastic animals and a doll from the home corner for the old lady.
3. Encourage students to retell the story.
4. Have the students observe the different animals.
5. Discuss which animals from the story actually do eat each other, and which don't. For example, spiders eat flies, but people don't eat flies!

Option:
Discuss food chains. Cut and paste pictures from old *National Geographic* magazines to create food chain posters.

I Know an Old Lady Who Swallowed a Fly
Snack Connection

EATING "SPIDERS" AND "FLIES" (MMM!)

Ingredients:
Large black gumdrops, thin black licorice strings, knife, cookie cutters, sugar-cookie dough

Directions:
1. Cut eight licorice string legs for each spider.
2. Let children push the legs into gumdrop bodies.
3. Using cookie cutters in the shapes of the animals in the song, let children cut shapes out of sugar-cookie dough and bake. Or purchase animal crackers.
4. Let the children eat their candy and cookies in the sequence the animals were eaten in the tale. The children can dramatically "die" at the end by collapsing to the floor.

I Know an Old Lady Who Swallowed a Fly
Resources

BOOKS

The Friends of Emily Culpepper by Ann and Harvey Coleridge (Putnam's, 1983).
When seeking companionship, a lonely old lady miniaturizes the postman, milkman, and plumber, placing them in jars around the house. Humorous illustrations enhance the tale.

Golly Gump Swallowed a Fly by Joanna Cole, illustrated by Bari Weissman (Parents', 1981).
A prize-winning "yawner" encounters increasing difficulties as he tries to get rid of the fly he accidentally swallowed. This is a perfect book to contrast with the classic song.

Happy Birthday, Grampie by Susan Pearson (Dial, 1987).
A granddaughter's love breaks through barriers of age, language, and blindness with a special birthday gift for her grandfather.

How Old Is Old? by Ann Combs, illustrated by J. J. Smith-Moore (Price, Stern, Sloan, 1987).
Alistar's grandfather uses examples from nature to explain that being old is a relative concept.

I Know a Lady by Charlotte Zolotow (Greenwillow, 1984).
This multi-generational book is sure to delight all audiences. Sally describes a loving and lovable old lady in her neighborhood who grows flowers, waves to children, and bakes cookies for them.

I Know an Old Lady Who Swallowed a Fly by Jan Pienkowski (Price, Stern, Sloan, 1989).
This version with pop-outs is very popular. It comes in several sizes.

I Know an Old Lady Who Swallowed a Fly by Glen Rounds (Holiday House, 1990).
This is a good choice when showing multiple versions of the folk song.

I Know an Old Lady Who Swallowed a Fly by Nadine Bernard Wescott (Little, Brown, 1980).
Cute pictures enhance this retelling of the popular song.

Old Black Fly by Jim Aylesworth (Scholastic, 1992).
This story tells of 26 terrible things that a fly did, in alphabetical order. The rhyme is catchy and the illustrations humorously inspired!

The Old Woman and Her Pig by Paul Galdone (McGraw, Hill, 1960).
Black and white and color illustrations tell this tale with a cumulative text of sequential events for the old woman.

Roger's Umbrella by Honest Dan'l Pinkwater, illustrated by James Marshall (Dutton, 1982).
In this story, Roger's umbrella becomes increasingly wild and out of control until he is taught by three old ladies how to talk to it.

Sing Me a Story by Jane Browne (Crown, 1991).
Features thirteen songs based on well-known nursery rhymes and fairy tales. Instructions for making action movements accompany each song, including those for the "Old Woman in a Basket."

There Was an Old Woman by Steven Kellogg (Parents', 1974).
This is a traditional version of the old woman with the peculiar eating habits.

You Can't Catch Me! by Joanne Oppenheim (Houghton Mifflin, 1986).
This cumulative text is told in rhyme with unusual illustrations depicting a pesky black fly who taunts all the animals, boasting they cannot catch him . . . until he bothers one too many.

Princess and the Pea

STORY SUMMARY

A young princess proves her royal lineage by being unable to sleep on a bed of mattresses that rest on one solitary pea. The wretched round causes her to toss and turn all night long, and this proves that she is a true and dainty princess.

SETTING THE STAGE: PASS THE PEAS!

Materials:

Construction paper, drawing paper, scissors, markers, crayons, gummy adhesive (such as "Hold It"), *Princess and the Pea* video (see Resources, p. 216), popcorn, mattresses, tennis balls, sleeping bags

Directions:

- Place a construction paper footboard on the wall to set the theme for this story.
- Let students draw pictures of princesses on mattress-shaped pieces of construction paper. Have the students pile their mattresses on the footboard and stick them to the wall with the gummy adhesive. A short ladder may be necessary as the bed grows higher and higher.
- Bedtime rituals are very important to young children. Discuss the important elements of these routines. Students can dictate their personal rituals and then illustrate them.
- If possible, bring several mattresses into the classroom and place them on the floor around the room. Use tennis balls for peas, and place one under each mattress. Have students enact the tale in small groups.
- Have a "slumber party" for part of the class session. Students can come in nightclothes and bring a bedroll or sleeping bag. Watch *The Princess and the Pea* video and serve popcorn.

The Princess and the Pea
Learning Connection

P IS FOR PRINCESS . . .

Introduce the students to words that begin with "P," such as princess, party, people, perfume, and paper. Have the children brainstorm as many "P" words as they can.

PRINCESS'S WRITING ASSIGNMENT

Duplicate the writing worksheet (p. 207) and give one to each child in the class. Have the children practice printing the letter "P" and words that begin with "P" by copying the examples given or by choosing words from the brainstormed list.

PRINCESS'S FOLDER

Duplicate the folder cover (p. 208) and give one to each child to color and glue to the front of a manila folder. Provide dried peas for children to glue to the bed. Children can also cut out princess patterns (p. 210) to glue to the bed.

Princess

party

P

p

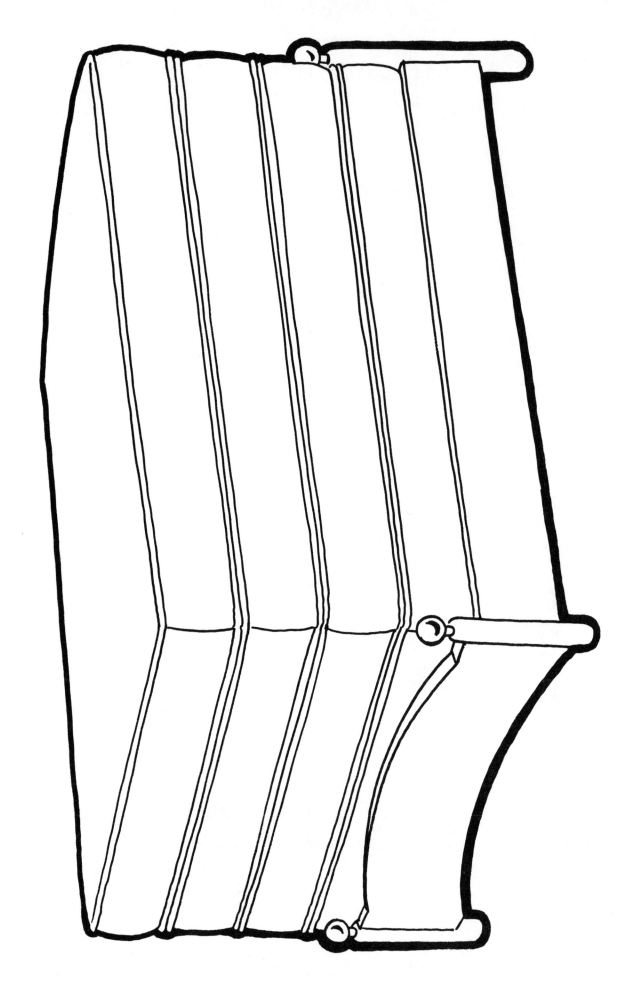

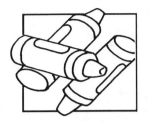

The Princess and the Pea
Art Connection

A BED FOR A PRINCESS

Materials:
Colored construction paper, princess patterns (p. 210), crayons or markers, shoe boxes (one per child), stapler or tape, shredded paper or fiberfill, dried peas, fabric scraps, scissors

Directions:
1. To make mattresses, have children fold sheets of construction paper in half.
2. They can staple or tape around two edges.
3. Provide scraps of paper or fiberfill for children to use to stuff the mattresses.
4. Give each child several dried peas to put into the mattress.
5. Have the children staple or tape the final edge closed.
6. To make pillows, have children repeat the above process, substituting small fabric pieces for the construction paper and leaving out the peas.
7. Provide shoe boxes for children to decorate for bed frames. They can put their mattresses and pillows inside the shoe boxes.
8. Give each child a copy of the princess pattern to color.
Encourage children to use the patterns and the mattresses to retell the story.

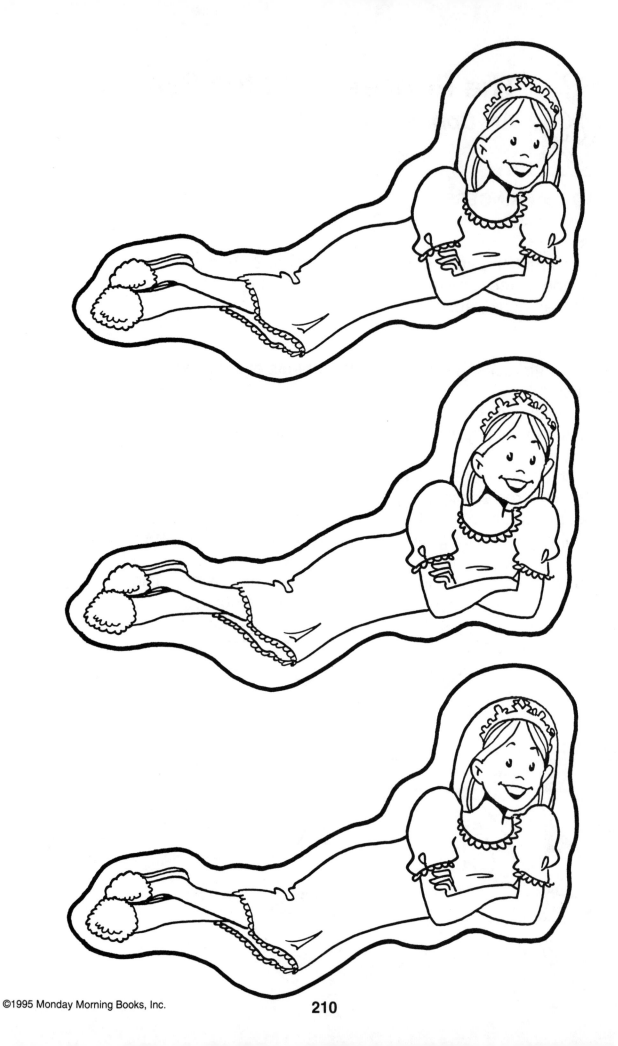

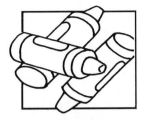

The Princess and the Pea
Art Connection

THE PAPER BAG PRINCESS

Materials:
Paper bags (one per child), scissors, crayons, markers, tempera paints, paintbrushes

Directions:
1. Read the *Paper Bag Princess* by Robert Munsch (Annick Press, 1980) to your students. In the story, a princess rescues a selfish prince, only to realize that she doesn't want to marry him after all.
2. Provide large paper grocery sacks for children to use to make paper bag apparel. Set out scissors, markers, crayons, and tempera paint and brushes for children to use for decorating their bags.
3. Reread the story to the class, and have children act out the parts. Designate a dragon, and let the rest of the students be paper bag princesses (and princes).

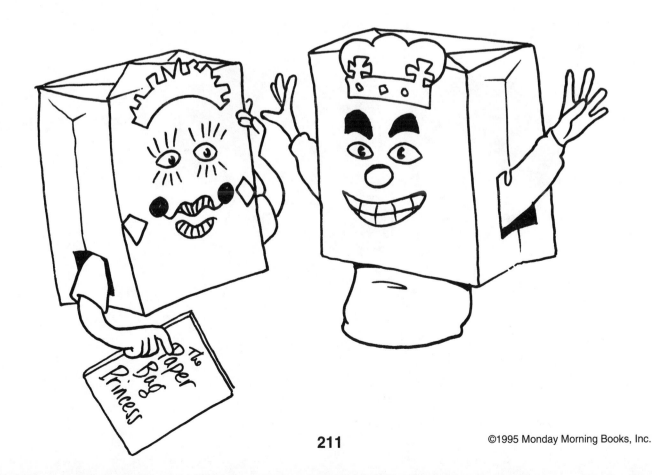

The Princess and the Pea
Math Connection

PLENTY OF PEAS!

Materials:
Clear containers in various sizes (with lids), dried peas, writing paper, pencil

Directions:
1. Fill a few clear containers with peas. (Make sure that the containers are in a range of sizes.)
2. Take estimations from each student as to how many peas are in each container. Write the estimations on a sheet of paper.
3. As a class, count out how many peas are in the smallest container.
4. Ask your students if anyone wants to revise his or her estimates for the larger containers.
5. Count out the peas in the rest of the containers.

Note: You may want to have children count over a dishpan or pail.

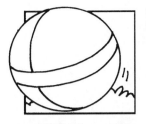

The Princess and the Pea
Games Connection

MAKING A BED

Materials:
Child's bed, strips of writing paper, marker, bedding

Directions:
1. Bring in a small child's bed.
2. Write all the words for the parts of the bed on sentence strips. For example: pillow, headboard, footboard, legs, frame, mattress, sheet, pillowcase, and so on.
3. Make a game with your students in which they label all the parts by placing the strips on and around the correct parts of the bed.
4. Demonstrate how to make the bed, and let each student have a chance to practice this self-help skill.

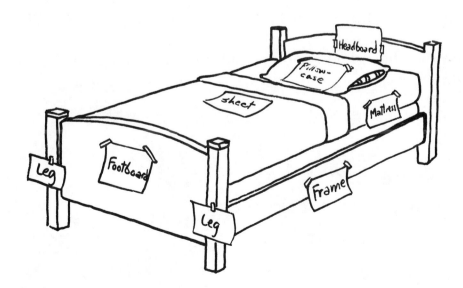

The Princess and the Pea
Snack Connection

PEAS PORRIDGE PLEASE!

Peas porridge hot
Peas porridge cold
Peas porridge in the pot
Nine days old.

Ingredients:

Cans of split pea soup (enough for the class), crackers, crock pot, small cups or bowls, spoons

Directions:

1. In a crock pot, heat up enough split pea soup so that every student can have a small taste.
2. Serve the soup with crackers.

PEAS FOR PRINCESSES (AND PRINCES, TOO)

Ingredients:
English peas

Directions:

1. If they are in season, buy English peas in the pod and let students shell them.
2. Either steam the shelled peas or let children eat them raw. (They're sweet and crunchy!)

Some like it hot,
some like it cold,
some like it in
the pot,
nine days old!

The Princess and the Pea
Resources

BOOKS

Angelina and the Princess by Katharine Holabird (Clarkson N. Potter, 1984).
Angelina is sick and loses out on the lead in the ballet to be performed for the princess, but at the last minute she gets her starring role. Adorable story and illustrations.

Ba Ba Sheep Wouldn't Go to Sleep by Dennis Panek (Orchard, 1988).
Ba Ba Sheep decides it would be fun to stay up all night and play, but he is so tired the next day that he looks forward to going to bed.

The Baby's Story Book by Kay Chorao (Dutton, 1985).
Includes fifteen familiar folk tales and fables with animals as the characters, short text, and sweet illustrations.

The Bed Book by Harriet Zeiffert (Scholastic, 1981).
A large-type phrase on each page describes the illustration of the bed.

The Cowboy and the Black Eyed Pea by Tony Johnston, illustrated by Warren Ludwig (Putnam's, 1992).
Farethee Well, the daughter of a Texas rancher, decides to test for a real cowboy by placing a pea under fifty saddle blankets!

Detective Whoo by Dennis Panek (Bradbury Press, 1981).
Strange noises disturb Detective Whoo's sleep and send him out into the night in search of the source.

Mother, Mother, I Want Another by Maria Polushkin (Crown, 1978).
Short text and darling illustrations depict an anxious mother trying to get her son what he wants in order to go to sleep. What he really wants is another kiss, not another mother.

The Night Book by Mark Strand (Clarkson N. Potter, 1985).
The rising moon sees a little girl who is afraid of the night. The moon sends down a special moonbeam to show her the many wondrous things to see during the dark hours.

One Bear at Bedtime: A Counting Book by Mick Inkpen (Little, 1987).
A little boy describes all the animals he needs to help him get ready for bed.

Paper Bag Princess by Robert Munsch (Annick Press, 1980).
After rescuing the prince, the princess realizes that he really is a bum and she has no desire to marry him after all. A new classic!

Pavo and the Princess by Evaline Ness (Scribner's, 1964).
This book is a great lesson on emotions with an unusual style of illustrations. It tells of a princess who never cried until the loss of Pavo, a favorite gift. However, the story does end happily.

Peace At Last by Jill Murphy (Dial, 1980).
Darling and colorfully illustrated pages depict Mr. Bear as he spends the night searching for enough peace and quiet to go to sleep.

The Princess and the Pea
Resources

The Princess and the Pea by Hans Christian Andersen (Houghton, 1978).
This story of a supersensitive princess is given a new look.

The Princess and the Pea by Hans Christian Andersen, illustrated by Dorothee Duntze (North-South Books, 1984).
Many beautiful, large illustrations tell this tale with a short text.

The Princess and the Pea by Hans Christian Andersen, illustrated by Janet Stevens (Scholastic, 1982).
Wonderful illustrations with animal characters and short text.

The Princess and the Pea by Hans Christian Andersen, illustrated by Dick Gackenbach (Macmillan, 1983).
A partial page of text for each of the darling illustrations. Not quite easy enough for the beginning reader.

Princess Pearly by Nicki Weiss (Greenwillow, 1986).
Rosemary is mean to her younger sister Pearl until she sees Pearl's friend act mean to her, too.

The Snow Rose by Sandra and Michel LaRoche (Holiday House, 1983).
A troubadour engages in a series of tests to win the hand of the princess, but as time passes he realizes there is a prize more precious than the cold-hearted princess. This is a nice book to include in the unit to contrast story lines.

The Stinky Cheese Man and other Fairly Stupid Tales by Jon Scieszka, illustrated by Lane Smith (Viking, 1992).
"The Princess and the Bowling Ball" is one of the silly retold tales in this very funny Caldecott Honor Book.

The Storybook Prince by Joanne Oppenheim (Harcourt, 1987).
A rhyming story in which no one can succeed in making the young prince go to sleep until an old woman tries with a bedtime story.

Ten Sleepy Sheep by Holly Keller (Greenwillow, 1983).
A fun book in which Lewis, while counting sheep to help him sleep, finds ten noisy sheep having a party in his bedroom.

A Visit to Sleep's House by Mary Pope Osborne (Knopf, 1989).
A child visits the house of sleep, where everything is quiet except for the river that whispers, "Good night, good night."

When Sheep Cannot Sleep: The Counting Book by Satoshi Kitamura (Farrar, Straus, 1986).
Cute illustrations and very brief text capture the difficulty of insomnia.

You Be Good and I'll be Night: Jump on the Bed Poems by Eve Merriam (Morrow, 1988).
This book includes thirty-five pages of brief, rhyming, illustrated poems.

OTHER
Princess and the Pea (CBS/Fox Video, 1984).
Part of the Faerie Tale Theatre series.

Queens

STORY SUMMARY

Queens are very important characters in fairy tales and nursery rhymes, at least as important as kings! There's the Queen of Hearts (who loves her tarts), and the queen who eats bread and honey (in "Sing a Song of Sixpence"). The Queen of Hearts also appears in *Alice's Adventures in Wonderland* (although she's not very nice). And there is an evil queen in *Snow White* (she's very vain) and in the *Snow Queen!* There are many queens who don't have names, but who play important roles, nonetheless. Ask your students to brainstorm as many queens as they can!

SETTING THE STAGE: QUEEN FOR A DAY

Materials:

Mirrors, red construction paper, scissors, glue, stapler, glitter, *The Snow Queen*, Styrofoam pellets

Directions:

- Have children discuss the different queens that they know. Ask them to name their favorites. Discuss what qualities make a queen a good ruler.
- Bring in several mirrors and have students chant: "Mirror, mirror on the wall, who's the fairest of them all?" Of course, all students are the "fairest" in their own way. (Note: Bring in a lighted make-up mirror. The children will be thrilled!)
- Invite students to come dressed as a character from their favorite "queen" story. If possible, have them bring the story to school with them. (Boys may dress as kings from fairy tales and rhymes.)
- Read a version of the Snow Queen tale, such as *The Snow Queen* by Amy Ehrlich, illustrated by Susan Jeffers (Dial, 1982). Use Styrofoam pellets as snowflakes, and have children pretend they have gone to the palace of the Snow Queen to rescue Kai.
- Provide red construction paper for children to use to make paper crowns with hearts on top, and let children act out the King and Queen of Hearts.

Queens
Learning Connection

Q IS FOR QUEEN . . .
Introduce the students to words that begin with "Q," such as queen, quiet, quick, quarrel, and quince. Have the children brainstorm as many "Q" words as they can.

QUEEN'S WRITING ASSIGNMENT
Duplicate the writing worksheet (p. 219) and give one to each child in the class. Have the children practice printing the letter "Q" and words that begin with "Q" by copying the examples given or by choosing from the list of brainstormed words.

QUEEN'S FOLDER
Duplicate the folder cover (p. 220) and give one to each child to color and glue to the front of a manila folder. Provide red crayons or markers (or heart-shaped stickers) for children to use to decorate the Queen of Hearts. Children can keep all the work from this unit in their folder.

Queen

quiet

Q

q

219

Queens
Mother Goose Connection

MOTHER GOOSE—FIT FOR A QUEEN!
Your students will be sure to love these Mother Goose rhymes. Read them at storytime. Or duplicate the Mother Goose poetry pattern page (p. 222), and give a copy to each child. Children can draw illustrations on the pattern pages to go with each Mother Goose rhyme.

THE QUEEN OF HEARTS
The Queen of Hearts
She made some tarts
All on a summer's day.
The Knave of Hearts
He stole the tarts
And took them clean away.

The King of Hearts
Called for the tarts,
And beat the knave full sore;
The Knave of Hearts
Brought back the tarts,
And vowed he'd steal no more!

PUSSY CAT, PUSSY CAT
Pussy cat, pussy cat, where have you been?
I've been to London to look at the queen.
Pussy cat, pussy cat, what did you there?
I frightened a little mouse under her chair.

HECTOR PROTECTOR
Hector Protector was dressed all in green,
Hector Protector was sent to the Queen.
The Queen did not like him,
No more did the King;
So Hector Protector was sent back again.

ROCK-A-BYE, BABY
Rock-a-bye, baby,
Thy cradle is green,
Father's a nobleman,
Mother's a queen;
And Betty's a lady,
And wears a gold ring,
And Johnny's a drummer,
And drums for the king.

Mother Goose Poetry Page

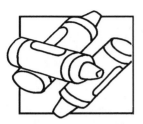

Queens
Art Connection

"SNOW" CASTLES

Materials:
Paper plates (one per child), sugar cubes, glue, glitter

Directions:
1. Let the children make "snow" structures by gluing sugar cubes onto paper plates.
2. Provide glue and silver glitter for children to use to drizzle over their completed structures to add a bit of sparkle.

Option:
Provide paper flags for children to glue to their snow castles.

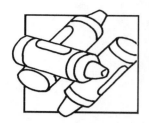

Queens
Art Connection

THE QUEEN'S HEARTS

Materials:
Queen of Hearts patterns (p. 225), pink and red construction paper, scissors, doilies, fabric scraps, ribbon, buttons, sequins, glitter, glue, marker, crayons

Directions:
1. Show the children how to fold the construction paper and cut out hearts. (Provide templates or stencils for younger children to use as models.)
2. Set out a selection of art materials for children to use to decorate their hearts. Doilies work well for backgrounds. Fabric scraps give the hearts added texture. Ribbon, buttons, sequins, and glitter add dimension to the hearts.
3. Give each child a copy of the Queen of Hearts pattern to cut out, color, and glue to a piece of construction paper as a background for his or her heart.
4. Let children dictate a message about their heart to you.
5. Post the hearts next to the dictations on a St. Valentine's bulletin board. (Cover the bulletin board first with heart-patterned fabric or wrapping paper for an interesting background.)

Option:
Have the children exchange the cards with friends.

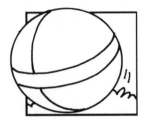

Queens
Games Connection

CARD CASTLES

Materials:
Decks of playing cards

Directions:
1. Have children help you sort out the face cards from several different decks.
2. Let the children match the cards by suits (or by decks if the backs are different).
3. Challenge the children to build a card castle, seeing how high they can make it before it falls down!

QUEEN, MAY I?

Directions:
1. Have the children play this game the same way as they would play "Mother, May I?"
2. Encourage students to use as much "royal" vocabulary in their requests as they can. They can create new kinds of steps to take, for example, "Queen, may I take six Knave of Heart steps?" (This might be a running step, since the Knave had to flee from the King of Hearts!)

Queen, may I take four steps?

Queens
Snack Connection

BREAD AND HONEY

Ingredients:
Bread, squeeze bottles of honey, milk

Directions:
1. This is a simple snack that children can make themselves. Give children a choice of plain bread or toast.
2. Provide squeeze bottles of honey for the children to use to coat their bread.
3. Serve with milk. Encourage the children to pretend to be the queen in the parlor, eating her bread and honey!

Option:
Set out peanut butter, too, for children to make PB & H sandwiches.

227

Queens
Resources

BOOKS

Michael Hague's Favourite Hans Christian Andersen Fairy Tales by Hans Christian Andersen (Holt, 1981).
This book includes nine favorite Andersen tales.

The Missing Tarts by B. G. Hennessy, illustrated by Tracey Campbell Pearson (Viking, 1989).
When the Queen of Hearts discovers that her strawberry tarts have been stolen, she enlists the help of many popular nursery rhyme characters in order to find them.

Rachel Fister's Blister by Amy MacDonald (Houghton Mifflin, 1990).
Rachel's blister sends adults hurrying for a cure, but nothing helps until the queen gives some advice.

The Snow Queen by Amy Ehrlich, illustrated by Susan Jeffers (Dial, 1982).
The illustrations make this book well worthwhile, despite long text.

The Wise Queen by Anthea Bell, illustrated by Chihiro Iwasaki (Picture Book Studio, 1984).
Beautiful illustrations add to the touching story of a girl who uses her cleverness to become, and remain, the queen.

OTHER

Snow Queen (CBS/Fox Video, 1983).
This Faerie Tale Theatre production features Melissa Gilbert, Lee Remick, Lauren Hutton, and others.

Rapunzel

STORY SUMMARY

A poor man's pregnant wife craves the salad greens that grow in the garden of her next door neighbor. Unfortunately, the neighbor is a witch, and she catches the man stealing her greens. The witch forces the man to give up his newborn daughter, Rapunzel, for her to raise. The witch imprisons lonely Rapunzel in a tower that has no door. The only way in or out is by climbing on Rapunzel's lovely hair. Luckily, a prince uses Rapunzel's long hair to come to her rescue.

SETTING THE STAGE: RADIANT RAPUNZEL

Materials:

Yellow yarn, scissors, corrugated paper with brick pattern, tape, scissors, witch's hat, crown

Directions:

- A lesson on braiding hair and yarn is intriguing to most students. Cut the lengths of yarn and knot them at the top. If you have a drawer at the appropriate height, insert the knotted end of the yarn into the drawer and shut it. Demonstrate how to braid the yarn, and then demonstrate again on a long-haired volunteer. (Separate the yarn or hair into three strands. Bring the left over the middle, the right over the middle, and repeat.) Younger students can simply twist yellow yarn.
- Invite a local hairdresser or barber into the class to do a demonstration for the students.
- Use corrugated brick paper to make several towers. Tape and roll the paper into tubes that are tall enough for a student to stand in. Make a long thick braid from yellow yarn and hang it from a window cut in the side of the tower. Let students take turns acting out characters in the story. (A witch's hat from Halloween is all the witch needs. And the prince can make do with a paper crown.)

Rapunzel
Learning Connection

R IS FOR RAPUNZEL . . .

Introduce the students to words that begin with "R," such as Rapunzel, rabbit, rain, race, and rat. Have the children brainstorm as many "R" words as they can.

RAPUNZEL'S WRITING ASSIGNMENT

Duplicate the writing worksheet (p. 231) and give one to each child in the class. Have the children practice printing the letter "R" and words that begin with "R" by copying the examples given or by choosing from the list of really radical brainstormed words.

RAPUNZEL'S FOLDER

Duplicate the folder cover (p. 232) and give one to each child to color and glue to the front of a manila folder. Provide yellow crayons for children to use to color Rapunzel's hair and red crayons for the bricks in the castle. Children can keep all the work from this unit in their folder.

Rapunzel

rain

R

r

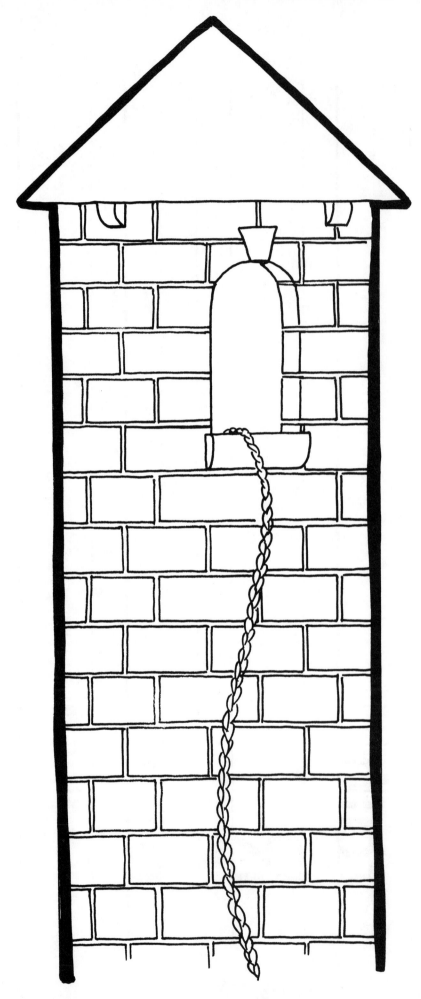

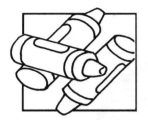

Rapunzel
Art Connection

RAPUNZEL'S TOWER
This is a desk-sized version of the paper towers described in "Setting the Stage."

Materials:
Rapunzel patterns (p. 234), red construction paper, crayons (including black), tape, yellow yarn, scissors, glue

Directions:
1. Let students make their own construction paper towers by rolling and taping sheets of colored paper. (Note: Children can use black crayons to draw bricks on the red paper before rolling it.)
2. Provide thin yellow yarn for them to braid and glue to a window cut into their tower.
3. Duplicate the prince and Rapunzel patterns for children to color and cut out. They can glue these characters to the tower or to sheets of construction paper to use as background.

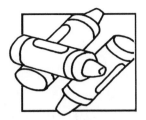

Rapunzel
Art Connection

A ROOM WITH A VIEW

Materials:
Large sheets of butcher paper, easels, scissors, tempera paint, paintbrushes

Directions:
1. Cut window shapes from butcher paper, either large rectangles or curved openings.
2. Clip the shapes to easels.
3. Have children imagine that they are trapped in a tower. Encourage them to paint the view from their solitary window.
4. Post the completed windows from a "Room with a View" bulletin board.

Option:
Check out books from the library with examples of the works of well-known landscape painters. This is the perfect opportunity to show a few famous prints.

Rapunzel
Math Connection

RED, BROWN, YELLOW, BLACK . . . BLUE?

Materials:
Hair patterns (p. 237), large sheet of paper, tape or glue, scissors, markers, crayons

Directions:
1. Make a graph of the different hair colors in the classroom, and how many there are of each color.
2. Duplicate and cut out the hair patterns for children to color to look like their own hair color and length.
3. Let children tape their pattern in the appropriate column on the graph.
4. Help children read the results of the graph.

Option:
Do a school-wide study of the students' hair colors.

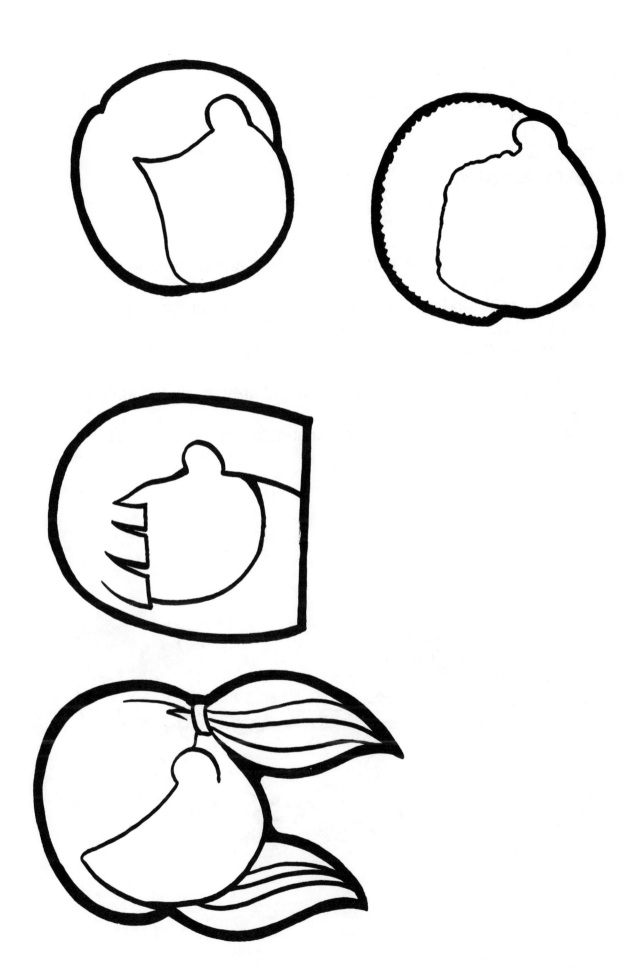

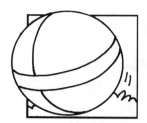

Rapunzel
Games Connection

RAPUNZEL PLAYGROUND
Turn your playground into a fairy tale set.

Directions:
- Children can climb the slide or jungle gym and pretend to be climbing Rapunzel's hair.
- A game of Tug-o-War (played with a rope) can be renamed "Tug-o-Hair."
- Children can use the merry-go-round to escape from the witch.
- If you have a garden, point out the salad greens like those that Rapunzel's father stole.
- Children can climb to the top of the jungle gym and look out from their "solitary window."

Rapunzel
Snack Connection

RAPUNZEL'S PASTA

Ingredients:
Spaghetti and bow-tie pasta, English muffins (half a muffin per child), sliced olives, red pepper strips

Directions:
1. Cook up a pot of long spaghetti noodles. (Option: Add a bit of yellow food coloring to the boiling water.)
2. Throw in a handful of bow-tie pasta, so that each child can decorate the "hair" on his or her plate with bows.
3. Toast English muffins and let children arrange the spaghetti hair around the muffin "heads."
4. For facial features, provide sliced olives for eyes and red pepper strips for mouths.

Rapunzel
Resources

BOOKS

An Enchanted Hair Tale by Alexis De Veaux (Harper and Row, 1987). Sudan suffers when people ridicule his strange-looking hair. However, he comes to accept and enjoy the enchantment.

If I Had Long, Long Hair by Angela Elwell Hunt (Abingdon, 1988). Loretta ponders the good and bad things that might happen if she had long, long hair. She finally decides that she likes being the way she is. But the process for her to get there is a long one!

Petrosinella: A Neapolitan Rapunzel by Giambattista Basile (Warne, 1981). This story is more gently told, with the ogre chasing a couple rather than the prince being blinded (as he is in the original story). This version provides an excellent opportunity to compare story lines.

Rapunzel by Bernadette Watts (Crowell, 1975). This book retells the story of the beautiful young girl imprisoned in a tower by a wicked witch.

Sleeping Beauty and Other Fairy Tales by Jacob and Wilhelm Grimm (Dover, 1992). Unabridged English translation of Rapunzel with black and white illustrations.

OTHER

Rapunzel (CBS/Fox Video, 1983). This Faerie Tale Theatre production features Jeff Bridges, Shelley Duvall, and Gena Rowlands.

Creative Teaching Press
Overhead Transparencies for Creative Dramatics
CTP 0301 Fairy Tales II (includes Rapunzel)

CTP
P.O. Box 6017
Cypress, CA 90630-0017

Sing a Song of Sixpence

STORY SUMMARY

Sing a song of sixpence
A pocket full of rye
Four and twenty blackbirds
Baked in a pie.
When the pie was opened,
The birds began to sing.
Wasn't that a dainty dish
To set before the King?

The King was in the counting house
Counting out his money.
The Queen was in the parlor
Eating bread and honey.
The maid was in the garden,
Hanging out the clothes,
When along came a blackbird
And snipped off her nose!!

SETTING THE STAGE: BEAUTIFUL BLACKBIRDS

Materials:
Clothesline, dress-up clothes, clothespins, English coins, paper crowns, apron, pie tin, false noses

Directions:
- String a clothesline across two chairs and have children hang dress-up clothes from the line using clothespins. (Show the children how to use the clothespins first. Discourage pinching.)
- Collect English coins (if possible) for children to observe. Discuss the value of the coins and the difference between English coins and American coins. Check out *Money* by Joe Cribb (Knopf, 1990).
- Set out props for the poem: crowns for the King and Queen, an apron for the maid, a pie tin for the blackbirds. Look for fake noses at costume or party shops to add to the props.

Sing a Song of Sixpence
Learning Connection

S IS FOR SING . . .
Introduce the students to words that begin with "S," such as sing, song, sixpence, story, snap, and supper. Have the children brainstorm as many super "S" words as they can.

SING ABOUT A WRITING ASSIGNMENT
Duplicate the writing worksheet (p. 243) and give one to each child in the class. Have the children practice printing the letter "S" and words that begin with "S" by copying the examples given or by choosing from the brainstormed vocabulary list.

SING ABOUT A FOLDER
Duplicate the folder cover (p. 244) and give one to each child to color and glue to the front of a manila folder. Provide feathers for children to glue to the blackbirds. Children can keep all the work from this unit in their folder.

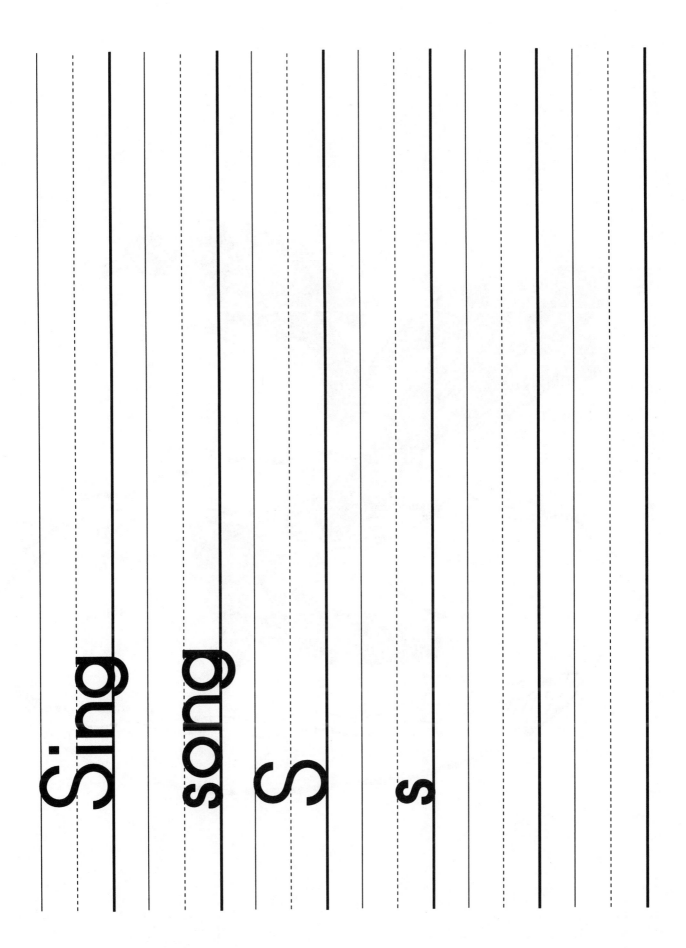

243

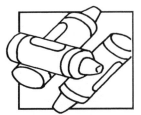

Sing a Song of Sixpence
Art Connection

CREATIVE CLOTHES

Materials:
Easel paper, easels, scissors, tempera paint, paintbrushes, clothes-line, clothespins, scissors

Directions:
1. Cut out clothing shapes from easel paper.
2. Post the cutouts on easels.
3. Provide tempera paints for children to use to paint the clothes.
4. Hang the completed clothes paintings from a clothesline strung in the hallway. Use clothespins to hang the artwork.

Option 1:
Set out old fashion magazines for children to look through before creating their own clothes designs.

Option 2:
Purchase paper dolls and paper doll clothes for children to experiment with. Dover Publications (31 East 2nd Street, Mineola, NY 11501) has inexpensive, old-fashioned paper dolls.

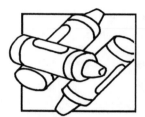

Sing a Song of Sixpence
Art Connection

PLAYDOUGH PIES

Materials:
Playdough, clay, sand, rolling pins, cookie cutters, spatulas, wooden spoons, garlic presses, and eggbeaters

Directions:
1. Let children choose their media to make pies. They can make clay or Playdough pies inside. Or let them make sand or mud pies at the sand table or in the sandbox.
2. Provide a variety of cooking utensils for children to use to mold their pies. Rolling pins, cookie cutters, spatulas, wooden spoons, garlic presses, and eggbeaters are all useful items.
3. Encourage children to serve their masterpieces to each other.

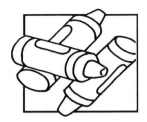

Sing a Song of Sixpence
Art Connection

FOUR AND TWENTY BLACKBIRDS

Materials:
Blackbird pattern (p. 248), sponges, scissors, large sheets of easel paper, tins of black tempera paint

Directions:
1. Use the blackbird pattern to cut bird shapes from sponges.
2. Show children how to dip the sponges in the tins of black paint and then press down on large sheets of easel paper cut into pie shapes (large circles big enough to fit 24 sponge-print blackbirds).
3. Help the children count their birds to make "four and twenty."

Option:
Use the rest of the story patterns (p. 249) to cut shapes from sponges. Provide other colors of tempera paint and additional pieces of paper and let children stamp out the story.

Sing a Song of Sixpence
Math Connection

SIXPENCE MATH

Directions:
- Have children look for groups of six items around the room and outside.
- Practice addition and subtraction facts to six.
- Make groups of four and twenty with items from your classroom, such as chairs, mats, blocks, dolls, stuffed animals, people, and so on.
- Make a pie chart on a large piece of paper of the children's favorite pies. Divide the chart to show the percentage of children who like blueberry, apple, cherry, pumpkin, peach, pecan . . . and blackbird pies!
- Provide coins for the kings (and queens) to count. Challenge the children to count out rows of four and twenty coins.

Option:
Share *Anno's Counting House* by Mitsumasa Anno (Philomel, 1982) with the children. (They can compare *Anno's Counting House* with the King's Counting House!) Anno's book follows ten children as they move from their old house into their new house with all of their possessions.

Sing a Song of Sixpence
Snack Connection

PLENTIFUL PIES

Ingredients:
Pre-made pie crusts, filling, milk

Directions:
1. Let children assist you in making easy pies from pre-made crusts.
2. Take a vote on the type of filling children would like to have. (Refer to your pie graph of favorite pies in "Sixpence Math.") You might suggest an apple pie with twenty-four raisins scattered inside to represent the blackbirds.
3. Bake according to directions on the package and serve with milk.

Sing a Song of Sixpence
Resources

BOOKS

Anno's Counting House by Mitsumasa Anno (Philomel, 1982).
Anno's goal is for children to gain a deep grasp of the correlation of abstract symbols and specific objects in their world. One by one, ten children move from their old house into their new house. Windows reveal the interiors of the houses. The book can also be read from back to front!

Money by Joe Cribb (Knopf, 1990).
This Eyewitness Book uses text and photographs to explore and examine the symbolic and material meaning of money. It discusses how money is made, as well as how to collect coins.

Money: A True Book by Benjamin Elkin (Children's Press, 1983).
This book discusses the history of money as a form of exchange in the world. Short text accompanies large photographs.

The Nose Book by Al Perkins (Random House, 1970).
Brief rhyming text and humorous illustrations in bright colors note that noses are interesting and serve many purposes.

Sing a Song of Sixpence by Randolph Caldecott (Barron's, 1988).
Originally published in 1880, this edition brings Caldecott's illustrations to a new generation of children. There is one line of text for each illustrated page.

Sing a Song of Sixpence by Tracey Campbell Pearson (Dutton, 1985).
A page of humorous and colorful pictures for each phrase of the traditional poem.

Sing a Song of Sixpence by Ed Southgate (Modern Curriculum Press, 1984).
A "Green Star" children's reader that features this favorite rhyme for beginning readers.

Sing a Song of Sixpence: A Favorite Mother Goose Rhyme by Leonard Lubin (Lothrop, 1987).
This illustrated version is set in the time of Henry VIII. Elaborately detailed illustrations include the Three Stooges as bakers. Each verse is set in a bordered page and followed by several pages of pictures.

Sing Me a Story by Jane Browne (Crown, 1991).
This book features thirteen songs based on well-known nursery rhymes and fairy tales. Instructions for making action movements accompany each song.

Thumbelina

STORY SUMMARY

A wish is granted to a woman who desperately wants a child. She plants barley corn from which a flower grows, and in the bloom is tiny Thumbelina. Unfortunately, Thumbelina is stolen away by a toad to marry his son. A fish, butterfly, and mouse all come to her assistance and save her from tragedy. Mole, who wants her for his wife, tells Thumbelina about a wounded bird. Thumbelina saves the bird, and the bird later repays the favor by rescuing her from marriage to the mole. Thumbelina ends up marrying the King of the Fairies and they live happily ever after.

SETTING THE STAGE: TERRIFIC THUMBELINA

Materials:
Miniature items, large and small object pairs

Directions:
- Ask the students to bring any miniatures or doll house furniture that they have at home for "Show and Tell." Display the miniature items on a table in the classroom.
- Set out paired extra large/extra small objects for the children to observe. Examples: a large work boot and a baby bootie, a ladle and a baby spoon, a "Big Book" and its trade-size copy.
- Discuss the terms "a rule of thumb," "thumbs up," and "thumbs down." Have children use the thumb symbols throughout the day.
- Encourage the students to try to imagine how their lives might be different if they were very small. Have the students pretend they are shrinking, and then walk around the room on their knees. Have them try to reach the toys and supplies they need from this position.

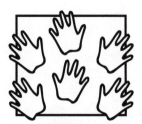

Thumbelina
Learning Connection

T IS FOR THUMBELINA . . .
Introduce the students to words that begin with "T," such as Thumbelina, thumb, tiny, teeny, teeth, and train. Have the children brainstorm as many terrific "T" words as they can.

THUMBELINA'S WRITING ASSIGNMENT
Duplicate the writing worksheet (p. 255) and give one to each child in the class. Have the children practice printing the letter "T" and words that begin with "T" by copying the examples given or by choosing from their totally "tubular" brainstormed words.

THUMBELINA'S FOLDER
Duplicate the folder cover (p. 256) and give one to each child to color and glue to the front of a manila folder. Provide pastel tissue paper squares for children to glue to the flower petals. Children can keep all the work from this unit in their folder.

Thumb

tiny

T

t

255

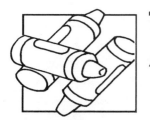

Thumbelina
Art Connection

THUMBELINA THUMB PRINTS

Materials:
Ink pads in various colors, white paper, thin-tipped markers, colored markers and crayons, tissue paper, embroidery thread, glue, scissors, fabric scraps, construction paper

Directions:
1. Show children how to use their fingertips to make prints on their papers.
2. Provide thin markers for children to use to draw features onto their prints.
3. Set out colored markers and crayons for children to use to draw clothes on their thumb print people. They can add embroidery thread hair, tissue paper or fabric scrap clothes, and cut out paper petals for nearby flowers.

257

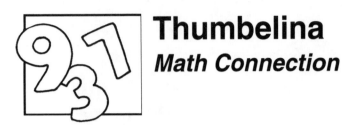

Thumbelina
Math Connection

RULE OF THUMB MATH

Materials:
Paper, pens, cardboard, scissors, lunch box, chair, paper, construction paper

Directions:
1. Have students measure items in the room by thumb lengths, using either their own thumbs or cut-out cardboard thumbs.
2. Make a chart of thumb lengths for items around the room, for example, lunch box, chair, paper.
3. Ask the children if they think measurements vary from thumb to thumb.
4. Have students trace around their thumb lengths on the same piece of construction paper to make a class thumb chart.
5. Have students compare and contrast their thumb shapes and sizes.

Thumbelina
Discovery Connection

MINIATURE MARVELS

Materials:
Clear plastic container, miniature items, birdseed, paper, marker, tape

Directions:
1. In a clear plastic container place multiple miniature items from craft, hobby, or novelty stores. Or use items from games, such as the tokens in Monopoly.
2. Make a list or a picture key of the items in the container.
3. Pour birdseed into the container until it is nearly full, allowing for shifting of contents. Shut securely and tape it closed.
4. Have students look for the items on the list (or picture key) as they turn the container.

©1995 Monday Morning Books, Inc.

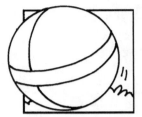

Thumbelina
Games Connection

PEANUT RELAY RACES

Materials:
Peanuts in the shell (one per child), thin-tipped marker, large spoons

Directions:
1. Draw a face on each peanut with a felt-tipped pen.
2. Divide the children into teams, and give each child a peanut and a large serving spoon.
3. Explain the rules of a relay race to the children. They will each carry a "Thumbelina" across the room until all team members have completed the course.

Option:
Let children draw faces on the peanuts themselves.

WHERE IS THUMBKIN?

How are you today, sir?

Very well, thank you!

Materials:
Felt-tip pens

Directions:
1. Draw faces on the children's thumbs or thumbnails with felt-tip pens.
2. Teach them how to do the finger play "Where Is Thumbkin?", which follows the tune "Frère Jacques." Children hold both hands behind their backs and sing, "Where is Thumbkin? Where is Thumbkin?" Then they bring out the first hand with the thumb extended and answer, "Here I am." They follow with the second hand (also with thumb extended) and echo, "Here I am." The first hand asks, "How are you today, sir?" The second one answers, "Very well, I thank you." And then both hands say, "Run away. Run away." The game can be repeated naming all the fingers (pointer, middle, ringie, pinkie).

Thumbelina
Snack Connection

DOLL-SIZED SNACKS

Materials:
Thinly sliced pieces of bread cut into quarters, thinly sliced cheese, mayonnaise and mustard, doll-sized plates and cups, water or juice

Directions:
1. Make teeny tiny snacks fit for Thumbelina. Let children eat tea sandwiches cut into bite-sized pieces from doll dishes.
2. Serve water or juice in doll-sized cups.
3. Have children pretend that they are small enough to suit the tiny tableware.

Thumbelina
Resources

BOOKS

The 46 Little Men by Jan Mogensen (Greenwillow, 1990).
This book relates in wordless illustrations the adventures of 46 little men who live in the pictures on the nursery wall. The final two pages of illustration list some characters by name, telling a little about them.

George Shrinks by William Joyce (Scholastic, 1985).
George dreams that he shrinks, and awakens to find that indeed he is small. This Reading Rainbow selection has short text and many humorous illustrations.

Issun Boshi, The Inchling by Momoko Ishii (Walker, 1965).
This is an old Japanese tale in which Issun Boshi, only an inch tall, becomes the attendant to the princess. After conquering demons trying to harm the princess, he is granted a wish and is made into a full-sized man.

Michael Hague's Favourite Hans Christian Andersen Fairy Tales by Hans Christian Andersen (Holt, 1981).
Includes nine favorite Andersen tales that are interspersed with full-page illustrations.

Sleeping Beauty and Other Fairy Tales by Jacob and Wilhelm Grimm (Dover, 1992).
Includes an unabridged English translation of Tom Thumb.

Sleeping Beauty and Other Favourite Fairy Tales by Angela Carter (Otter Books, 1991).
English translation of the Charles Perrault version of Hop o' My Thumb.

Thumbelina by Hans Christian Andersen, illustrated by Adrienne Adams (Scribner's, 1961).
Read this book over a few days, or summarize the story for the children. Show the delightful pictures while you read or tell the story.

Thumbelina by Hans Christian Andersen (Doubleday, 1990).
The illustrations by Alison Claire Darke have created a vibrant new version of this classic tale about the tiny heroine, Thumbelina.

Thumbelina by Hans Christian Andersen, illustrated by Petula Stone (Lady Bird Books, 1992).
This classic fairy tale is beautifully illustrated and produced in a miniature size.

Thumbelina and the Prince adapted by Francine Hughes from a screenplay by Don Bluth (Grosset and Dunlap, 1994).
This is a more modern version of the classic tale.

OTHER

Thumbelina read by Kelly McGillis, music by Van Dyke Parks, illustrated by Diana Bryan (Rabbit Ears Production).

 # **U**gly Duckling

STORY SUMMARY
Other animals make fun of the poor ugly duckling (an egg mislaid). But the little misfit has the last laugh—he grows up to be a beautiful swan!

SETTING THE STAGE: DELIGHTFUL DUCKLINGS

Materials:
Paper pad, marker, construction paper (yellow, gray, white), scissors, glue

Directions:
- Make a chart listing the differences and similarities between ducklings and cygnets (baby swans).
- If possible, plan a field trip to a local lake or petting zoo to see ducklings and cygnets.
- Discuss the words "vanity" and "vain" in regards to the animals who made fun of the poor duckling.
- Divide the class into small groups so that they can reenact the story. Make simple props of yellow, gray, and white paper wings and beaks. After the children act out the story, hold a discussion about how it feels to be picked on. Ask the children how it felt when they were "ugly" and how they felt when they were "beautiful."
- For a comparison of stories, read "The Really Ugly Duckling," a short story in *The Stinky Cheese Man and Other Fairly Stupid Tales* by Jon Scieszka, illustrated by Lane Smith (Viking, 1992).

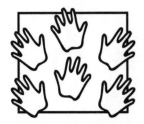

The Ugly Duckling
Learning Connection

U IS FOR UGLY . . .

Introduce the students to words that begin with "U," such as ugly, under, umbrella, umpire, and underwear. Have the children brainstorm as many "U" words as they can.

UGLY DUCKLING'S WRITING ASSIGNMENT

Duplicate the writing worksheet (p. 265) and give one to each child in the class. Have the children practice printing the letter "U" and words that begin with "U" by copying the examples given or by choosing unique words from their brainstormed list.

UGLY DUCKLING'S FOLDER

Duplicate the folder cover (p. 266) and give one to each child to color and glue to the front of a manila folder. Provide feathers for children to glue to the duck patterns. Children can keep all the work from this unit in their folder.

under, umbrella, use, umpire, up, ukulele...

Ugly

under

U

u

265

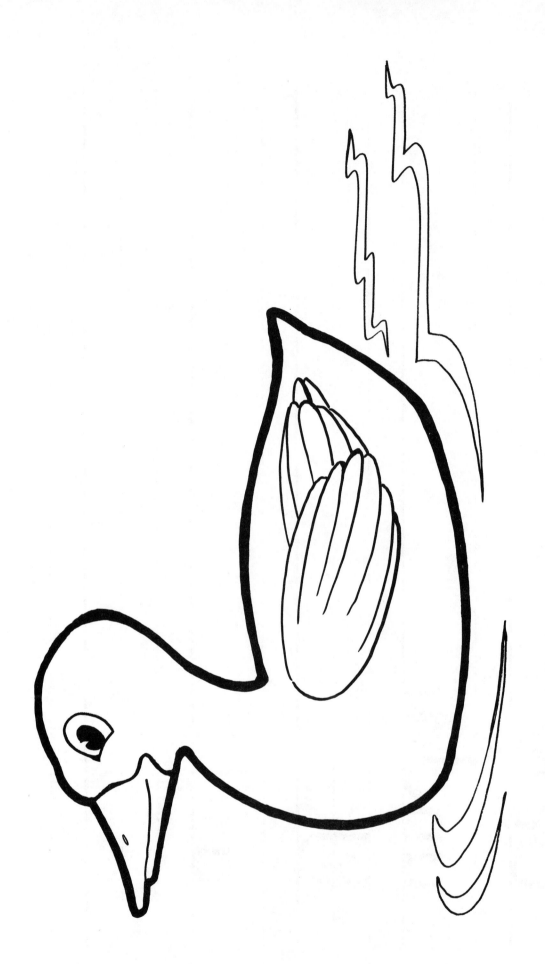

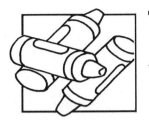

The Ugly Duckling
Art Connection

NESTING DUCKS

Materials:
Duck patterns (p. 268), shredded paper, small paper bowls, oak tag or tagboard, scissors, glue, feathers, colored construction paper, markers

Directions:
1. Duplicate the patterns onto oak tag or tagboard and give one to each child to color and cut out.
2. The children can glue feathers to the duck patterns.
3. Give each child a paper bowl and shredded paper to use to build nests for the ducks.
4. Help children cut out construction paper eggs to fit into their nests. They can decorate the eggs with markers. You can provide oval-shaped stencils from tagboard for the children to use.

The Ugly Duckling
Discovery Connection

RUBBER DUCKIES

Materials:
Blue food coloring, rubber ducks, water table

Directions:
1. Add blue food coloring to the water table.
2. Place rubber ducks in the water table.
3. Let the children use the ducks to reenact the story of the Ugly Duckling.

Note: Rubber ducks are often available in different sizes. If possible, buy both ducklings and grownup sizes.

Option:
Read to the students from *Ducks Don't Get Wet* by Augusta Goldin, illustrated by Leonard Kessler (Crowell, 1989). This is a "Let's Read and Find Out Science Book" that describes the habits and behaviors of ducks. It emphasizes the physical characteristics that prevent ducks from getting wet. Or read *The Little Ducks* by Judy Dunn, photos by Phoebe Dunn (Random House, 1976). This book has short text and excellent photos.

The Ugly Duckling
Math Connection

SORTING EGGS

Materials:
Small plastic Easter eggs, egg cartons, tempera paint, paintbrushes

Directions:
1. Have the children sort the plastic eggs by colors.
2. If possible, set out eggs of different sizes for children to sort. They can sort by color and size.
3. Set out egg cartons with a circle of color painted in the bottom of each section.
4. Have the children set the same colored egg on top of the correctly colored dot in each section.

Option:
For a math extension, number the egg carton sections and number the eggs (using markers or removable stickers). Have children match the plastic eggs to the numbered carton.

The Ugly Duckling
Snack Connection

EGG-CITING EGGS

Materials:
Eggs, Easter egg dyes

Directions:
1. Hard boil an egg for each child.
2. Provide dyes for children to use to color the eggshells.
3. When children have finished dying their eggs, help them peel the shells, dip the eggs in salt and pepper, and eat them.

Option 1:
Read *The Easter Egg Farm* by Mary Jane Such (Scholastic, 1992) while the children dye their eggs.

Option 2:
Make egg salad for the children and serve it with crackers.

The Ugly Duckling
Resources

BOOKS

The Easter Egg Farm by Mary Jane Such (Scholastic, 1992).
Vibrantly colored illustrations enhance the story of an unusual chicken that lays amazing eggs. The eggs look like whatever the chicken saw while she was laying them. (Her chicks turn out unusual as well!)

Make Way for Ducklings by Robert McCloskey (Scholastic, 1941).
A duck family travels through town looking for a place to live. With brown and white illustrations. This is a Caldecott Award Book.

Michael Hague's Favourite Hans Christian Andersen Fairy Tales by Hans Christian Andersen (Holt, 1981).
Includes nine favorite Andersen tales that are interspersed with illustrations.

Once Upon a Time Tales: The Ugly Duckling by Jane Jerrard (New Seasons Publishing, 1992).
There is a page of text opposite each page of illustrations in this small book that tells the traditional tale.

The Stinky Cheese Man and Other Fairly Stupid Tales by Jon Scieszka, illustrated by Lane Smith (Viking, 1992).
The story of "The Really Ugly Duckling" is a very funny retelling of the classic story.

The Ugly Duckling by Hans Christian Andersen, illustrated by Adrienne Adams (Charles Scribner's Sons, 1965).
Nice, pastel illustrations accompany long text.

The Ugly Duckling by Hans Christian Andersen, illustrated by Monika Laimgruber (Greenwillow, 1982).
This is a beautifully done version of the traditional tale. An ugly and unloved duckling turns out to be a beautiful swan. Intricate borders surround all pages with full pages of detailed illustrations.

The Ugly Duckling by Hans Christian Andersen, retold by Marianna Mayer, with illustrations by Thomas Locker.
This version is written for grades K-3.

The Ugly Duckling by Hans Christian Andersen, retold by Lillian Moore, illustrated by Daniel Dan Soucci (Scholastic, 1987).
Even though the text is somewhat long, the illustrations will draw students along through the story.

The Ugly Duckling by Joel Tuer and Clara Stites, illustrated by Robert Van Nutt (Knopf, 1986).
A modestly updated, strikingly illustrated edition of the classic.

The Ugly Duckling by Hans Christian Andersen (Weekly Reader, 1985).
The traditional tale is geared towards a primary reader.

The Wild Swans by Hans Christian Andersen, retold by Amy Ehrlich, illustrated by Susan Jeffers (Dial, 1981).
The purity of a gentle princess triumphs over evil.

OTHER

The Ugly Duckling (Rabbit Ears Production).

Hans Christian Andersen's The Ugly Duckling by Hans Christian Andersen, read by Peter Bartlett and Barbara Bliss (Durkin Hayes, 1994).
This cassette is part of the "Classic Tales" series.

(Rip) Van Winkle

STORY SUMMARY
Rip Van Winkle is a hen-pecked husband who wanders into the Catskill Mountains. On his walk he meets some strange men, and he drinks from their flagon. He falls asleep and when he wakes up, he goes back home where nobody recognizes him. To the poor man's dismay, he discovers that his nap lasted 20 years!

SETTING THE STAGE: VERY SLEEPY VAN WINKLE

Materials:
Butcher paper, marker, plastic or metal container, time capsule memorabilia, baby photos of students, old photo of yourself, mirror, gray beard

Directions:
- On a sheet of butcher paper, make a time line. List a few of the most important events that happened in the last twenty years. Choose events that you think would be especially meaningful to your students, such as landing a man on the moon and creating VCRs.
- Discuss your own childhood with your students. Tell them what life was like before home computers, portable telephones, and CD players. Next, have the children work with you to make predictions of changes that may happen in the next twenty years.
- Make a time capsule of a few of the children's favorite items for a future generation to find. Have a ceremony to bury the capsule somewhere on campus. (Use a plastic or metal container to hold the items.)
- Ask students to bring in their baby pictures. Encourage them to look at the pictures and then observe their reflections in a mirror. Have them notice how much they've changed in only a few years. Astound your students by bringing in a photo of what you looked like twenty years ago!
- Put a gray beard in the dress-up corner for children to put on when reenacting Rip Van Winkle's story.

Rip Van Winkle
Learning Connection

V IS FOR VAN WINKLE . . .

Introduce the students to words that begin with "V," such as visor, van, and vote. Have the children brainstorm as many "V" words as they can.

VAN WINKLE'S WRITING ASSIGNMENT

Duplicate the writing worksheet (p. 275) and give one to each child in the class. Have the children practice printing the letter "V" and words that begin with "V" by copying the examples given or by choosing from their very vibrant brainstormed vocabulary list.

VAN WINKLE'S FOLDER

Duplicate the folder cover (p. 276) and give one to each child to color and glue to the front of a manila folder. Provide cotton balls for children to glue to Rip Van Winkle's long, long beard. Children can keep all the work from this unit in their folder.

Van

vote

V

v

275

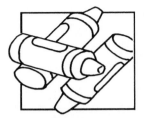

Rip Van Winkle
Art Connection

THEN AND NOW

Materials:
Tempera paint, paintbrushes, paper, current photographs of the children's back yards

Directions:
1. Have students paint pictures of what their back yard might have looked like twenty years ago. Students who don't have a yard could paint pictures of what the playground or a local park might have looked like.
2. Get children started on this assignment by discussing how places change over time. Have children help brainstorm ways that places change, for example, buildings are built, trees are chopped down, weeds are removed, roads are paved.
3. If possible, have children bring in photographs to school of what their yards look like now.
4. Post the paintings next to the photographs in a "Then and Now" display on your bulletin board.

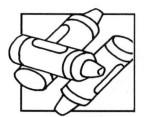

Rip Van Winkle
Art Connection

RIP VAN APPLE

Materials:
Apples, plastic knives with rounded edges, newsprint, paper towel (or toilet paper) tubes cut into short sections, scissors, markers or crayons, fabric scraps, glue, pipe cleaners

Directions:
1. Ask each student to bring an apple to school.
2. Using plastic knives, have children carve faces into the apples.
3. Set the apples on a newsprint-covered table and leave them until they shrivel. (Shriveling should take place within a week.)
4. Give each child a short paper towel or toilet paper tube section to decorate for Rip's body and glue to the apple head. Children can use markers, crayons, or fabric scraps to make Rip's clothing and pipe cleaners for his arms and legs. Assemble.

Rip Van Winkle
Math Connection

TWENTY-TWENTY

Materials:
Small bags, assorted small items (twenty of each)

Directions:
1. Plan to begin this unit on the twentieth day of the month or on the twentieth day of school.
2. Ask each student to bring twenty of several small items to school in a bag for counting practice. Examples: They can bring in twenty paper clips, twenty pennies, twenty jelly beans, and so on. (Have a few bags of twenty items on hand for children who forget theirs.)
3. Have children practice counting by twenties. They can work together and count the items in their own bag and in a friend's bag.

Rip Van Winkle
Discovery Connection

THE WONDER OF THUNDER

Materials:
Book on causes of thunder, such as *Crash, Rumble and Roll* by Franklyn M. Branley, illustrated by Barbara and Ed Emberly (Harper and Row, 1985).

Directions:
1. Thunder is a natural topic to discuss in conjunction with this story. Many young children are frightened by thunder. Ask the children in your class if any are afraid of thunder. If so, ask them to list reasons that make it frightening.
2. Discuss the many myths about the cause of thunder. Example: the gods are bowling.
3. Discuss the real cause of thunder, and read to children from *Crash, Rumble and Roll*.
4. Have your students brainstorm things they can do during a storm so that they are less frightened. Examples: Put a pillow over their ears (if they're scared of the loud noise). Have a flashlight on hand (if they're afraid the lights might go out). Count the seconds between the lightning and the thunder to find out how many miles away the storm is. Children can practice counting "One hippopotamus, two hippopotamus" to give a more accurate count for a second.
5. Discuss what to do if caught outside during an electrical storm. Tell children that they should not go under a tree for shelter and that they should not touch metal objects.

Option:
Follow up with the picture book *Rumble Thumble Boom* by Anna Grossnickle Hines (Greenwillow, 1992). This is an especially soothing book to read on a rainy day.

Rip Van Winkle
Math Connection

COUNTING ON HIPPOS

Materials:
Gray construction paper, hippopotamus pattern (p. 282), scissors, glue, round foam pieces

Directions:
1. Duplicate the hippopotamus head patterns onto gray construction paper.
2. Let children glue round foam pieces to the patterns for teeth.
3. Have the children line up the hippopotamus heads and then practice counting hippopotamuses between a flash of pretend lightning (flash the lights in the classroom) and thunder (clap hands).

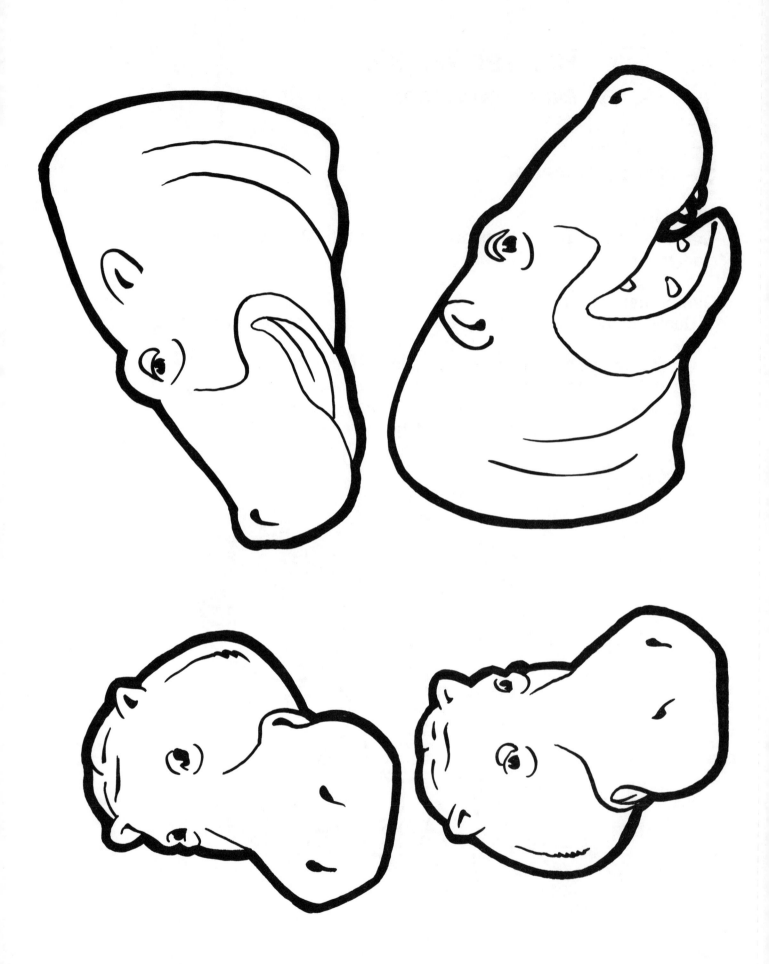

Rip Van Winkle
Dramatic Play Connection

WAKE UP, WINKLE!

Materials:
Paper grocery bag, pair of men's pants and a man's shirt, shredded newspaper, cotton, glue, markers, construction paper, scissors, safety pins

Directions:
1. Stuff a grocery bag with shredded paper and decorate it to look like Rip's head using markers or cutouts from construction paper. (You can add a cotton beard.)
2. Stuff a man's shirt and pants with shredded paper.
3. Attach the paper bag head to the body using safety pins.
4. Lay Rip down in a corner of the classroom. (Lean him against an overturned wastebasket for a stump.)
5. Have children take turns pretending to wake him up. They can also read him books, or lie down and pretend to go to sleep next to him.

Wake up! Wake up!

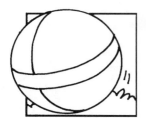

Rip Van Winkle
Games Connection

LAZY DAYS

Directions:
1. Have children lie down on mats and pretend to go to sleep.
2. When they "wake up" tell them that they have been sleeping for twenty years!
3. Ask the children to think about what Rip might have done when he first woke up. Ask if they think he was tired or full of energy.
4. Hold a stretching session. Have children touch their toes and do jumping jacks to help wake their bodies up!

BOWL-A-RAMA

Directions:
Nine pins (which the strange men play in the story) is similar to bowling. If possible, take children on a field trip to a local bowling alley. Let them watch an adult bowl and listen to the thunderous noise. Then provide a child-size set of plastic bowling pins and balls and let children play this game in the classroom.

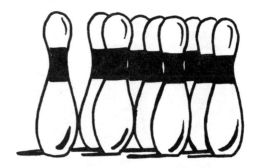

Rip Van Winkle
Snack Connection

TASTY TORTILLAS

Ingredients:
Small flour or corn tortillas, chopped olives, shredded cheese, alfalfa sprouts, sliced red peppers, sliced tomatoes, cucumber rounds, aluminum foil, permanent marker

Directions:
1. Give each child a tortilla to use for Rip's face.
2. Provide an assortment of toppings that the children can use to add features. For example, beards can be made from sprouts, shredded cheese, chopped olives, etc.
3. Lightly bake the tortillas on foil-covered pans to melt the cheese.

Note: Write each child's name on the aluminum foil next to his or her tortilla using a permanent marker. This will help you return each tortilla man to its rightful owner.

Rip Van Winkle
Resources

BOOKS

Crash, Rumble and Roll by Franklyn M. Branley, illustrated by Barbara and Ed Emberly (Harper and Row, 1985).
The book explains in a simple and direct way how and why a thunderstorm occurs. It gives safety steps to follow when lightning is flashing. A read-along tape is available.

Hippo Thunder by Susan Sussman, illustrated by John C. Wallner (Whitman, 1982).
A family helps a child to overcome the fear of a thunderstorm.

The Legend of Sleepy Hollow and Rip Van Winkle by Washington Irving (Franklin Watts, 1967).
This version is complete and un-abridged, with large-type text.

One Minute Bedtime Stories by Shari Lewis (Doubleday, 1982).
"Rip Van Winkle" is one of the twenty one-minute bedtime tales.

Rip Van Winkle by Washington Irving (Franklin Watts, 1966).
This version includes interesting historical notes.

Rolling by Matt Novak (Bradbury Press, 1986).
Fearful animals run from sounds of thunder, but they're led back home by a young boy with a drum.

Rumble Thumble Boom by Anna Grossnickle Hines (Greenwillow, 1992).
A boy and his dog Hercules come to terms with their fear of thunder. This is a soothing picture book to read during a thunder shower.

Thunder Cake by Patricia Polacco (Scholastic, 1990).
Grandma helps a young girl on the farm gather the ingredients for Thunder Cake as a storm approaches.

Tyler Toad and the Thunder by Robert L. Crowe (Dutton, 1980).
None of the animals' explanations for the origin of thunder reassures the frightened T. Tyler Toad. He decides to hide in a hole to wait for the storm to pass.

OTHER

Rip Van Winkle (CBS/Fox Video, 1985).
This Faerie Tale Theatre production features Harry Dean Stanton and Talia Shire and was directed by Francis Coppola.

Rip Van Winkle read by Angelica Huston, music by Jay Unjar, illustrated by Rick Meyerowitz (Rabbit Ears Productions).
Angelica Huston's reading creates convincing characters and uses humor to enhance the mood and setting. This cassette includes original music in the flavor of the time setting. It is the winner of a Parents' Choice Award.

 # **W**ild Swans

STORY SUMMARY

A young princess desperately wants to save her eleven brothers, who have been transformed into swans. In order to break the spell, she must knit them each a sweater made from stinging nettles. She is not allowed to speak until her task is complete, but even though she is silent a king falls in love with her. Still, even he is not able to protect her from the local people who decide that she is evil. They are about to put her to death when her brothers appear and shield her. She throws a sweater around each one, turning them all back into men. Unfortunately, the last sweater has only one arm finished, and her youngest brother spends the rest of his life with one human arm and one swan wing.

SETTING THE STAGE: SUPER SWANS

Materials:
Old sheet, scissors, diaper pins, green felt, wordless books, stopwatch

Directions:
- Cut up an old white sheet to make wings for eleven wild swans. You can pin the simple wing shapes to children's clothes with diaper pins. Encourage groups of children to reenact the story for each other. They will need eleven children for swans, one for the princess, one for the witch who casts the spell, and one for the king who falls in love with the princess. Scraps of green felt work well for the stinging nettles.
- Emphasize the fact that while the princess was unable to speak, she still could communicate. Set out a selection of your wordless books at a learning station, or highlight them in your class library. Challenge the students to see how long they can remain speechless. You can even time them using a stopwatch.
- Invite an adult into class to show children how to knit.
- Plan a field trip to watch swans swim at a local park or zoo.
- Invite an expert "signer" into the classroom to show children simple examples of sign language. See Resources (p. 296) for books on sign language.

©1995 Monday Morning Books, Inc.

The Wild Swans
Learning Connection

W IS FOR WILD . . .

Introduce the students to words that begin with "W," such as wild, water, weaving, words, and wonder. Have the children brainstorm as many wonderful "W" words as they can.

WILD SWAN'S WRITING ASSIGNMENT

Duplicate the writing worksheet (p. 289) and give one to each child in the class. Have the children practice printing the letter "W" and words that begin with "W" by copying the examples given or by choosing wild and wonderful "W" words from their brainstormed vocabulary list.

WILD SWAN'S FOLDER

Duplicate the folder cover (p. 290) and give one to each child to color and glue to the front of a manila folder. Provide white feathers for the children to glue to the swans and green felt or nylon net for children to glue on for the nettles. Children can keep all the work from this unit in their folder.

Wild
water
W
w

289

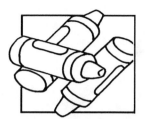

The Wild Swans
Art Connection

SWAN MOBILES

Materials:
Swan patterns (p. 292), construction paper, oak tag or tagboard, hole punch, yarn, scissors, crayons, markers, glue, glitter, feathers, wire hangers

Directions:
1. Duplicate the patterns onto heavy construction paper, oak tag, or tagboard and cut out.
2. Help children punch a hole in the top of each pattern.
3. Provide crayons, markers, glue, feathers, and glitter for children to use to decorate the mobile patterns.
4. Help children thread lengths of yarn through the holes and tie the patterns to hangers.
5. Provide colored construction paper in wild shapes for children to use to cover the body of the hanger.

The Wild Swans
Math Connection

SWAN GRAPHS

Materials:
Bird patterns (p. 294), crayons, markers, easel paper, scissors, glue

Directions:
1. Duplicate and cut out the bird patterns for children to color.
2. Have the children decide which type of bird is their favorite.
3. Make a graph on a large sheet of easel paper separated into columns.
4. Invite the children one at a time to place their favorite bird cutout in the appropriate column.
5. Help children read the results of the graph.

Option:
Set out books on birds in the book nook for children to read and look through. Choose from the following resources:
- *Amazing Birds* by Alexandra Parsons, photos by Jerry Young (Knopf, 1990). This is part of the "Eyewitness Juniors" series.
- *Bird* by David Burnie (Knopf, 1988). This is in the "Eyewitness" series.
- *Birds: A Guide to the Most Familiar American Birds* by Herbert S. Zim and Ira N. Gabrielson, illustrated by James Gordon Irving (Golden Press, 1956).
- *The How and Why Wonder Book of Birds* by Robert Mathewson, illustrated by Walter Ferguson and Ned Smith (Price, Stern, Sloan, 1981).
- *Ruth Heller's Designs for Coloring: BIRDS* (Grosset & Dunlap, 1990).
- *Zoo Books: Birds of Prey* (Wildlife, 1980).

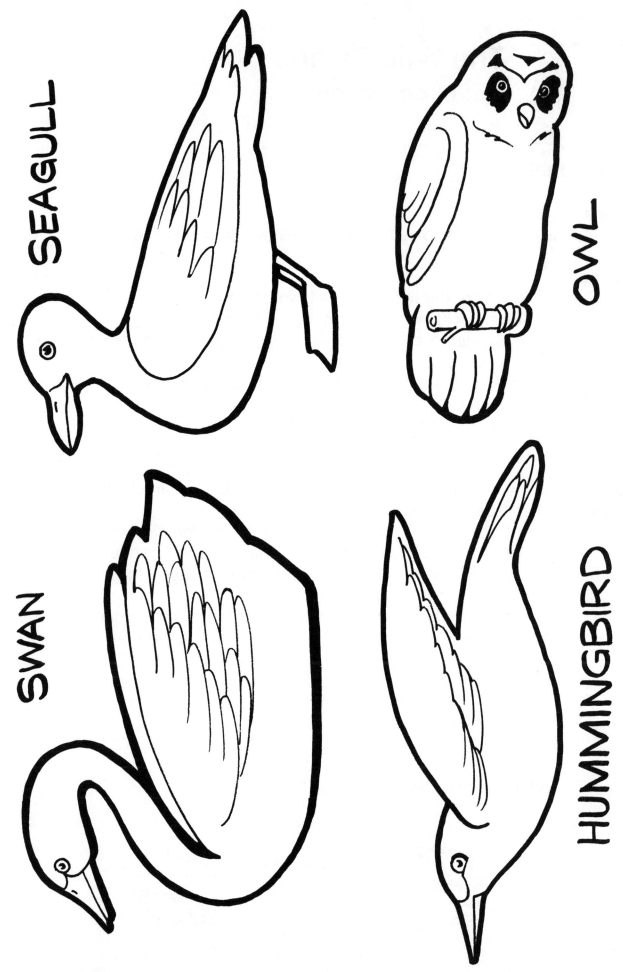

SEAGULL

OWL

SWAN

HUMMINGBIRD

The Wild Swans
Snack Connection

WORD-Y SOUP

Materials:
Vegetable soup with alphabet noodles, grated cheese, small bowls, spoons

Directions:
1. Give each child a bowl of vegetable soup that has plenty of alphabet noodles.
2. Have children try to make words from the letters in their vegetable soup.
3. Serve the soup with grated cheese.

Option 1:
Serve cereal that comes in the shape of letters. Have children spell out words with the cereal letters (on a sheet of aluminum foil) before they pour them in a bowl and eat them.

Option 2:
Read *Alphabet Soup* by Kate Banks, illustrated by Peter Sis (Knopf, 1988). A boy's ability to spell words with his alphabet soup comes in handy during the magical journey he takes with a friendly bear. Or read *Alpha Beta Chowder* by Jeanne Steig, illustrated by William Steig (HarperCollins, 1992). Each of the twenty-six verses tells a tale filled with savory words.

The Wild Swans
Resources

BOOKS

Michael Hague's Favourite Hans Christian Andersen Fairy Tales by Hans Christian Andersen (Holt, 1981).
This book includes nine of Andersen's favorite tales, including the story of the wild swans.

Sign Language Fun with Linda Bove (Random House, 1980).
This Sesame Street book presents sign language words grouped into usable categories (time, family, emotions).

Sign Language Fun with Linda Bove (Random House, 1985).
This Sesame Street book uses the residents of Sesame Street to introduce the letters of the alphabet in sign and pictures.

The Six Swans by Wanda Gag, illustrated by Margot Tomes (Coward, 1974).
A wicked enchantress tricks a king into marrying her, then, in a fit of jealousy, turns his six young sons into swans.

Swan Sky by Tejima Keizaburo (Philomel, 1988).
Despite the devoted attentions of her family, a young swan is unable to accompany them on the journey to their summer home. Outstanding illustrations accompany a short text.

The Wild Swans by Hans Christian Andersen, illustrated by Marcia Brown (Scribner's, 1963).
This version may be too long to read all at once to the children. Read it to get an idea of the story, and then retell it in your own words, showing the pictures to the children.

The Wild Swans by Hans Christian Andersen, retold by Amy Ehrlich, illustrated by Susan Jeffers (Dial, 1981).
This version has long text but outstanding illustrations.

The Wild Swans by Hans Christian Andersen, translated by Naomi Lewis, illustrated by Angela Barrett (Peter Bedrick Books, 1990).
Eleven princes who have been turned into swans are saved by their sister.

 # Fo**X** in Socks

STORY SUMMARY

Dr. Seuss' *Fox in Socks* (Random House, 1965) presents a truly silly collection of tongue twisters for children of all ages.

SETTING THE STAGE: FANTASTIC FOXES

Materials:

Wrapping paper, tape, empty boxes, scissors, stickers, ribbons, tape recorder, tape

Directions:

- Provide wrapping paper and empty boxes in various sizes for children to use to practice gift wrapping. They can decorate their wrapped boxes with ribbons or stickers. Read *The Gift* by John Prater (Viking, 1985) while they wrap their assorted boxes.
- Have the children take off their shoes and walk around in only their socks. They can sit in a circle while you read *Fox in Socks* to them.
- Have the children compare and contrast each other's socks. They can observe patterns, colors, solids, stripes, tights, and anklets (and bare feet if anyone forgot to wear socks!).
- Make a tape recording of the children saying tongue twisters. Play it over for them so that they can practice until they master the tricky sayings. *A Twister of Twists, A Tangler of Tongues* by Alvin Schwartz, illustrated by Glen Rounds (Bantam, 1977), is a great resource. It includes such twisty teasers as "The sixth sheik's sixth sheep's sick" and "A tooter who tooted a flute, tried to tutor two tutors to toot. Said the two to the tutor, 'Is it harder to toot or to tutor two tutors to toot?'"

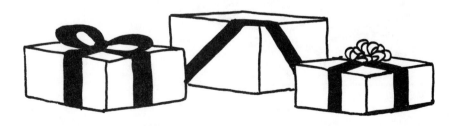

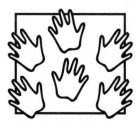

Fox in Socks
Learning Connection

X IS FOR . . .

Introduce the students to words that begin or end with "X," such as X-ray, xylophone, box, fox, and lox. Have the children brainstorm as many "X" words as they can. If they can't think of any others, have them say words that rhyme with "X" words.

FOX'S WRITING ASSIGNMENT

Duplicate the writing worksheet (p. 299) and give one to each child in the class. Have the children practice printing the letter "X" and words that begin or end with "X" by copying the examples given or by choosing from their "excellent" list of brainstormed words.

FOX'S FOLDER

Duplicate the folder cover (p. 300) and give one to each child to color and glue to the front of a manila folder. Provide scraps of fabric and felt for children to glue to the folder for socks. Let them use wrapping paper scraps to cover the boxes on the folder cover. Children can keep all the work from this unit in their folder.

X-ray

xylophone

X

x

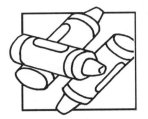

Fox in Socks
Art Connection

KIDS IN SOCKS

Materials:
Old socks, buttons, markers, felt scraps, yarn, glue, threaded plastic darning needles, wiggly eyes (optional)

Directions:
1. Have each student bring an old sock from home.
2. Set out buttons, markers, felt scraps, yarn, glue, and threaded plastic darning needles. Children also love to use large wiggly eyes (optional).
3. Let each student make his or her own puppet out of the sock.

Option 1:
Knee socks can be stuffed, tied, and decorated to look like snakes.

Option 2:
Knee socks can also be stuffed and pinned to belt loops for fox tails.

Fox in Socks
Math Connection

TONGUE TWISTER MATH

Materials:
Patterns (pp. 303-304), scissors, heavy paper, markers and crayons, tongue-twister book (optional)

Directions:
1. Duplicate the patterns onto heavy paper and cut out.
2. Let children color and decorate the patterns.
3. Read number-themed tongue twisters to your class, such as "The sixth sheik's sixth sheep's sick," "Six slippery seals slipping silently to shore," "Six selfish shellfish," or "Eight gray geese gazing gaily into Greece."
4. Have children use the patterns to reenact the tongue twisters.
5. Encourage children to try to make up their own numerical tongue twisters.

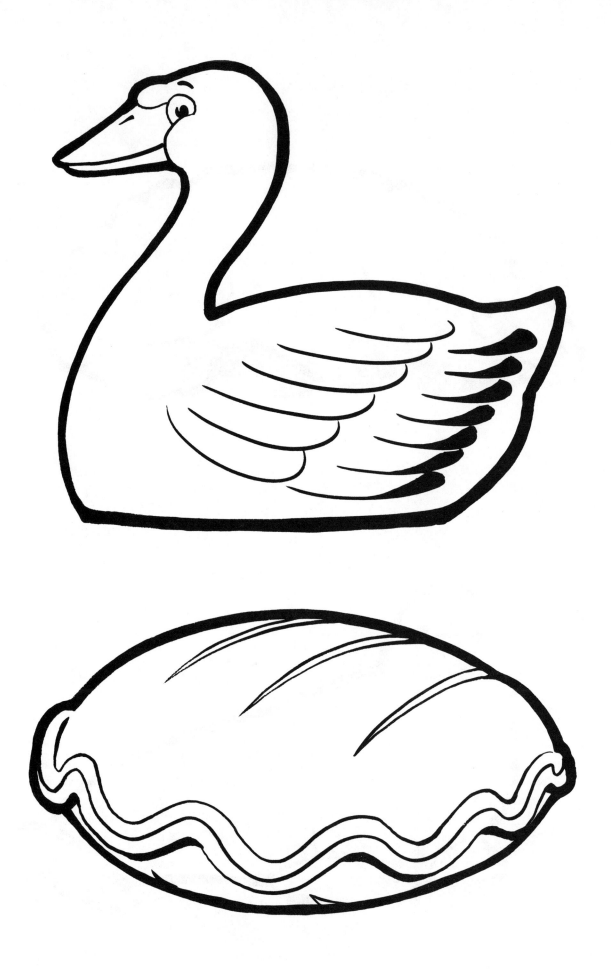

Fox in Socks
Snack Connection

X MARKS THE SPOT!

Materials:
Biscuit dough, aluminum foil, baking tins, rolling pins, permanent marker

Directions:
1. Purchase canned biscuit dough or biscuit mix and give each student enough dough to form a biscuit.
2. Have the children divide the biscuit dough in half and roll out the dough into two equal lengths.
3. Show students how to lay one piece of the dough on top of the other, crossing in the middle to form an "X."
4. Bake the biscuits according to directions on the package.

Note: To keep track of which "X" is which, bake the biscuits on a foil-covered pan and write each student's initials on the foil with a permanent marker.

Fox in Socks
Resources

BOOKS

An ABC Bestiary by Deborah Blackwell (Farrar, 1989).
Three-word tongue twisters underneath each vibrantly illustrated action animal, topped by both capital and lower-case letters.

Faint Frogs Feeling Feverish and Other Terrifically Tantalizing Tongue Twisters by L. Obligado (Puffin, 1983).
Animals of all types fill this book of tongue twisters.

Fantastic Mr. Fox by Roald Dahl (Knopf, 1970).
The three farmers in this book are each meaner than the other. They try to outdo each other in their all-out warfare to get rid of the fox and his family.

Fox in Socks by Dr. Seuss (Random House, 1965).
The fox in socks presents his rubber-tongue collection of brain-numbing twisters.

Fox's Dream by Tejima (Scholastic, 1987).
A fox in the icy-cold winter yearns for companionship and spring. The short text is greatly enhanced in true picture book format with hauntingly beautiful illustrations, which contrast markedly with the whimsical illustrations in the Seuss book.

The Gift by John Prater (Viking, 1985).
This is a wordless book about two children's imaginations and how they pretend with a box that their grandfather brought them.

Just a Box? by Goldie Taub Chernoff (Scholastic, 1971).
A how-to book for making imaginative play toys from household containers.

The Piggy in the Puddle by Charlotte Pomerantz, illustrated by James Marshall (Macmillan, 1974).
A tongue-twisting text is enhanced by humorous illustrations as the little piggy jumps in the middle of a mud puddle. Her parents and brother soon follow suit.

Sitting in My Box by Dee Lillegard (Dutton, 1989).
A box grows more and more crowded with animals until a hungry flea arrives.

There Are Rocks in My Socks Said the Ox to the Fox by Patricia Thomas (Lothrop, 1979).
Both color and black and white illustrations alternate in this "ox-y" text.

Timid Timothy's Tongue Twisters by Dick Gackenbach (Holiday House, 1986).
Two lines of tongue-twisting text for every brightly colored, silly, and immensely appealing illustration.

Tongue Twisters by Charles Keller, illustrated by Ron Fritz (Simon and Schuster, 1989).
Humorous illustrations enhance this collection of tongue twisters and hard-to-say rhymes.

A Twister of Twists, A Tangler of Tongues by Alvin Schwartz, illustrated by Glen Rounds (Bantam, 1977).
Very funny book of tongue twisters. A perfect resource for teachers.

# Yetta the Trickster

STORY SUMMARY

The main character in *Yetta the Trickster* by Andrea Griffing Zimmerman (Seabury, 1978) loves to play tricks on others, but sometimes the trick backfires and she winds up the butt of the joke! Tricks include "bonking" passers-by with apples, pretending she cannot hear, scaring people, and skimming off milk to sell for herself.

SETTING THE STAGE: TRICKY TRICKSTERS

Materials:
Plastic apples, serving spoons

Directions:
- Discuss the difference between fun tricks and tricks that are mean, dangerous, or harmful. Set firm boundaries in your classroom. Ask the children to think about whether they would be happy or unhappy to have a trick played on them.
- Discuss April Fool's Day. Tell the children that in different countries, there are different April Fool's Day customs. In England, April Fool's tricks are played in the morning. "Noddies" are people who fall for these tricks. In Scotland, these people are called "gowks," which is the name for a cuckoo bird. In France, they call the people "April Fish!" In Portugal, people celebrate the holiday on the Sunday and Monday before Lent by throwing flour at each other. Ask if any of the children's family has a traditional way to celebrate April Fool's Day.
- Read *Yetta the Trickster* and have the children pretend to be Yetta. Ask them to talk by moving their lips only, since Yetta pretended that she couldn't hear.
- Have a group of children act out the chapter in which Yetta scares the villagers.
- Hold relay races with plastic apples. Divide the children into teams and give each team an apple on a large serving spoon. On the word "Bonk," each member with a spoon races to a set destination and back, passing the spoon and the apple to the next student in line. Play until every student has an opportunity to race.

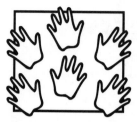

Yetta the Trickster
Learning Connection

Y IS FOR YETTA . . .
Introduce the students to words that begin with "Y," such as Yetta, yellow, yo-yo, and young. Have the children brainstorm as many "Y" words as they can.

YETTA'S WRITING ASSIGNMENT
Duplicate the writing worksheet (p. 309) and give one to each child in the class. Have the children practice printing the letter "Y" and words that begin with "Y" by copying the examples given or by choosing from their list of brainstormed vocabulary words.

YETTA'S FOLDER
Duplicate the folder cover (p. 310) and give one to each child to color and glue to the front of a manila folder. Children can keep all the work from this unit in their folder.

Yetta

yo-yo

Y

y

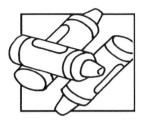

Yetta the Trickster
Art Connection

BONKING YETTA!

Naughty Yetta bonks people with apples. Have your students "bonk" their papers with apples to make prints.

Materials:

Apples cut in halves, pie tins of tempera paint (red and green), large sheets of paper

Directions:

1. Show children how to dip their apple halves in the paint and then press them down onto the paper to make prints.
2. Children can alternate dipping apples in red paint and green paint and make patterns with the different colors.
3. Encourage students to "bonk" only the paper and not each other!

Option:

Read from *Apples: How They Grow* by Bruce McMillan (Houghton Mifflin, 1979). This book describes how apples grow, from bud to ripe fruit.

Yetta the Trickster
Math Connection

APPLE MATH

Materials:
Cleaned seeds from apple cores (either from apples used at snack time or from apples used for printing—see "Bonking Yetta!"), whole apples

Directions:
1. Have children observe the apple seeds.
2. Ask them to guess how many seeds are in an apple.
3. Cut open an apple and have children count the seeds.
4. Cut open another apple widthwise and show children the star pattern that's inside.
5. Serve the apples at snack time.

Yetta the Trickster
Snack Connection

YETTA'S BUTTER
Yetta saved some of the milk each day to sell because she wanted to buy butter molds for her mother.

Ingredients:
Small container with a tight-fitting lid, whipping cream, fresh bread or muffins, milk

Directions:
1. Pour some whipping cream into a small container with a tight lid.
2. Allow each student to have an opportunity to shake the container.
3. Tell the students that they are making their own butter.
4. When the cream has become butter, spread it on fresh bread or muffins and serve it to the children so that they can taste the fruits of their labor.
5. Serve milk with the snack.

Option:
Serve the snack with apples cut in star shapes.

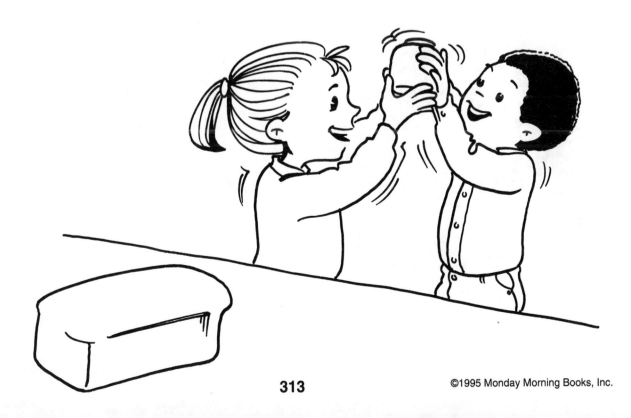

Yetta the Trickster
Resources

BOOKS

Arthur's April Fool by Marc Brown (Trumpet Club, 1983).
Arthur uses his brain to outsmart a bully on April Fool's Day. Fans of the Arthur stories will love this adventure.

Iktomi and the Berries by Paul Goble (Orchard Books, 1989).
This book relates Iktomi's fruitless efforts to pick some buffalo berries. This is the second in a series of books by Goble about Ikto, a Plains Indian legendary trickster.

Stone Soup by Ann McGovern, illustrated by Winslow Pinne Pils (Scholastic, 1986).
This is the tale of a young boy who tricks an old woman into making a wonderful soup for the two of them.

The Trickster by Gail Robinson (Atheneum, 1982).
A collection of nine Northwest Indian tales about Raven, the trickster who loves to get the better of others, but is also willing to help those in danger or distress.

Trickster Tales by I. G. Edmonds (Lippincott, 1966).
Eighteen tricksters from different cultures are depicted in this great teacher resource book.

The Trickster's Handbook by Peter Eldin (Sterling, 1989).
Ninety-six fun pages of illustrated tricks, jokes, and stunts that students will love to try.

Yetta the Trickster by Andrea Griffing Zimmerman (Seabury, 1978).
Four short chapters describe the jokes that Yetta loves to play on others. Of course, one day the joke is on her.

Zoos

STORY SUMMARY
"Oh! They would put me in the zoo, if they could see what I can do!" A crazy creature from Robert Lopshire's *Put Me in the Zoo* (Random House, 1960) wants to be in the zoo, but the circus is a better place for the talented performer.

SETTING THE STAGE: ZANY ZOOS

Materials:
Gift boxes, adhesive labels, hole punches, colored paper scraps, adhesive circular stickers (in a variety of colors), costumes, musical instruments, mirror

Directions:
- Have each child bring a small gift box to school. Provide markers and sticky labels for children to use to designate the containers as their "spot box." Set out a variety of hole punches (that make different shaped cutouts) and colorful paper scraps. Let children fill their boxes with spots.
- After reading *Put Me in the Zoo*, give each student a sheet of adhesive colored spots (available at stationery supply stores). The children can stick the spots on their clothes, but remind them to always collect the spots from where they put them. Place a mirror nearby for the children to look at themselves covered in spots.
- Hold a class talent show for other classes or for parents. Set out costumes and musical instruments, and let children perform whatever skill they feel comfortable with. For example, they might tap dance, sing a song (as a trio), show a painting, read a story, and so on. Shy children might want to form a group and perform together.
- Discuss zoos and wildlife parks. If possible, take a field trip to visit the animals. Or invite a zoo keeper to come to the classroom and speak to the children.

Zoos
Learning Connection

Z IS FOR ZOO . . .
Introduce the students to words that begin with "Z," such as zoo, zany, zebra, and zipper. Have the children brainstorm as many "Z" words as they can.

ZANY WRITING ASSIGNMENT
Duplicate the writing worksheet (p. 317) and give one to each child in the class. Have the children practice printing the letter "Z" and words that begin with "Z" by copying the examples given or by choosing zany words from their brainstormed vocabulary list.

ZOO KEEPER'S FOLDER
Duplicate the folder cover (p. 318) and give one to each child to color and glue to the front of a manila folder. Provide felt scraps and yarn for children to glue to the animals to give their folders a three-dimensional feel. Children can keep all the work from this unit in their folder.

Zoo

zebra

Z

z

317

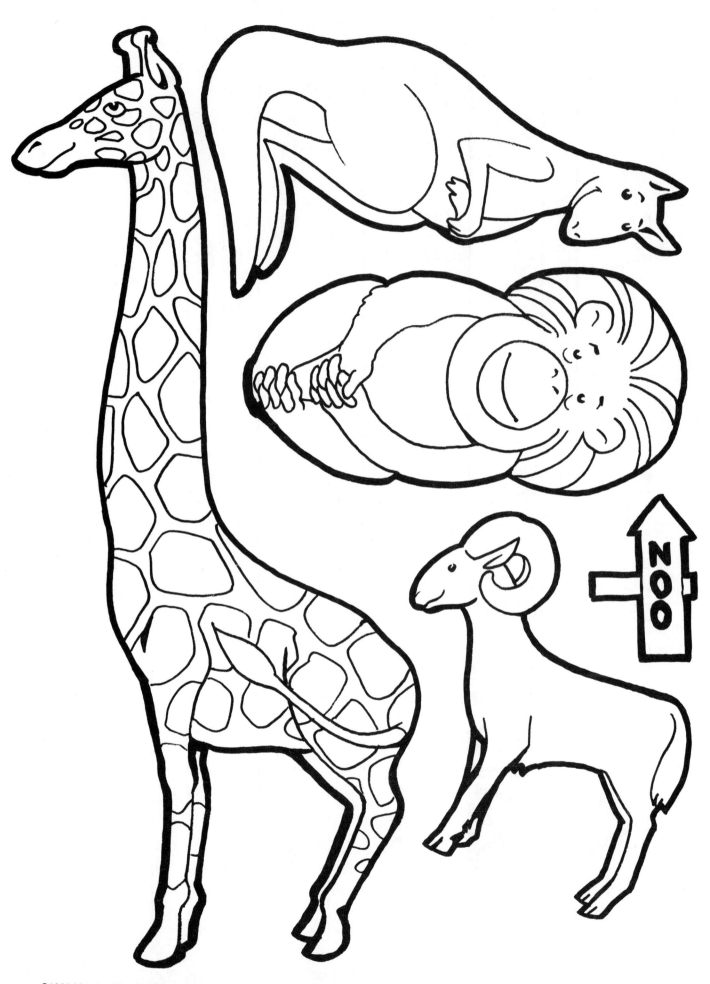

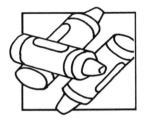

Zoos
Art Connection

SPOTTY ART

Materials:
Colored construction paper cut into large circles, tempera paint in pie tins, empty spools (and other small round objects to paint with), easels

Directions:
1. Put brightly colored circles of paper at the easels.
2. Provide empty spools and other circular objects for children to use to make multicolored spots on the papers.

PIZZA WITH SPOTS

Ingredients:
English muffins, tomato sauce, olives, tomato slices, cheese slices, pepperoni, aluminum foil, permanent marker, oven, cookie sheets

Directions:
1. Have children make miniature pizzas on English muffin halves covered with tomato sauce.
2. Set out only round toppings for the children to choose from, for example, sliced olives, tomatoes, pepperoni, and circles of cheese.
3. Heat the pizzas for 8 to 10 minutes at 425 degrees.

Note: Cook pizzas on aluminum foil-covered tins. Write children's initials on the foil next to their pizza to insure that each spotty pizza returns to its rightful owner.

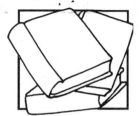

Put Me in the Zoo
Resources

A Children's Zoo by Tana Hoban (Greenwillow, 1985).
This book is perfect for young preschoolers to beginning readers since Hoban's color photographs of animals are accompanied by several descriptive words.

Circus Heros and Heroines by Rhina Kirk (Hamond, 1972).
Brief profiles of famous circus personalities accompany a short history of the circus.

One, Two, Three to the Zoo: A Counting Book by Eric Carle (Trumpet, 1968).
Large illustrations of zoo animals are done in Carle's unique style. A small train cumulatively grows at the bottom of each double-page illustration.

Paddington at the Zoo by Michael Bond (Putnam's, 1985).
Paddington feeds all six of the sandwiches he made to the zoo animals.

Polar Bear, Polar Bear, What Do You Hear? by Bill Martin, illustrated by Eric Carle (Holt, 1991).
This story shows zoo animals from the polar bear to the walrus making distinctive sounds for each other while children imitate the sounds of the zoo keeper.

Put Me in the Zoo by Robert Lopshire (Random House, 1960).
A crazy creature stars in this story. He wants to live in a zoo, but with all of his tricks he really belongs in the circus.

What Do You Do at a Petting Zoo? by Hana Machotka (Morrow, 1990).
This book features color photographs, mini-puzzles, and facts about the many animals found in a petting zoo.

Zoo by Anthony Browne (Knopf, 1992).
A boy endures a tedious visit to the zoo with his family.

A Zoo for Mister Muster by Arnold Lobel (Harper, 1962).
Mister Muster becomes assistant zoo keeper after all the animals pay him a midnight visit. The fun continues in the next book, *A Holiday for Mister Muster*, when he takes the animals for field trips on a picnic, to the beach, and to an amusement park.

Zoo Where Are You? by Ann McGovern, illustrated by Ezra Jack Keats (Harper & Row, 1964).
There are no zoos near Josh, so he decides to collect animals for one himself. He doesn't find animals, but he picks up a variety of treasures along the way. He is very proud of his "zooful of junk."

Zoos Without Cages by Judith E. Rinard (National Geographic, 1992).
Fascinating photos with kid appeal accompany factual information.